Our reading list.

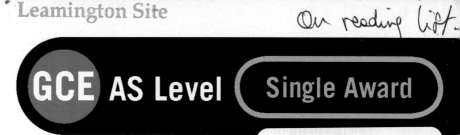

GCE AS Level · Single Award

D0185602

AS Level for AQA

Health & Social Care

Series editor

Neil Moonie

www.heinemann.co.uk

✓ Free online support
✓ Useful weblinks
✓ 24 hour online ordering

01865 888058

Heinemann

Inspiring generations

Heinemann Educational Publishers
Halley Court, Jordan Hill, Oxford OX2 8EJ
Part of Harcourt Education

Heinemann is a registered trademark of
Harcourt Education Limited

© Neil Moonie, Sian Lavers, Dee Spencer-Perkins, Beryl Stretch, 2005

First published 2005

10 09 08 07 06 05
10 9 8 7 6 5 4 3 2 1

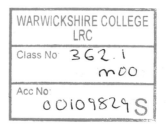

British Library Cataloguing in Publication Data is available
from the British Library on request.

10-digit ISBN: 0 435471 56 2
13-digit ISBN: 978 0 435471 56 9

Edited by Neil Moonie
Designed by Lorraine Inglis
Typeset and illustrated by Techtype

Original illustrations © Harcourt Education Limited, 2005

Cover design by Wooden Ark Studios

Printed by Scotprint Ltd

Cover photo: © Getty Images

Acknowledgements
Every effort has been made to contact copyright holders of material reproduced in this book. Any omissions will be
rectified in subsequent printings if notice is given to the publishers.

Websites
There are links to relevant websites in this book. In order to ensure that the links are up to date, that the links work,
and that the sites are not inadvertently linked to sites that could be considered offensive, we have made the links
available on the Heinemann website at www.heinemann.co.uk/hotlinks. When you access the site the express code
is 1562P.

Please note that the examples of websites suggested in this book were up to date at the time of writing. It is essential
for tutors to preview each site before using it to ensure that the URL is still accurate and the content is appropriate.
We suggest that tutors bookmark useful sites and consider enabling students to access them through the school or
college intranet.

Contents

Introduction to the 2005 edition   v

Acknowledgements   vi

Unit 1 Effective caring

    1.1   Life quality factors   2

    1.2   Treating people well   15

    1.3   Caring skills and techniques   23

    1.4   Services   31

    1.5   Access to services   37

    1.6   Rights and responsibilties of service users   40

    1.7   Risks and safe working   42

Unit 2 Effective communication

    2.1   Types of communication   50

    2.2   Communication difficulties and strategies to overcome
these   56

    2.3   Barriers to communication and factors affecting the
effectiveness of communication skills   58

    2.4   Communication when working in teams   63

    2.5   Clients and care settings   66

    2.6   Giving a talk   81

    2.7   Feedback research   91

    2.8   Evaluating communication skills   94

Unit 3 Health, illness and disease

3.1	Concepts of health and ill-health	100
3.2	Factors affecting health and well-being	104
3.3	Immunisation against disease	114
3.4	The value of screening	121

Answers to assessment questions   133

Glossary   135

Index   138

Introduction

This book has been written to support students who are studying for the single award AS level GCE using the course structure designed by AQA. The book is designed to support the three AS level units:

Unit 1 Effective caring (externally assessed)
Unit 2 Effective communication (internally assessed)
Unit 3 Health, illness and disease (internally assessed)

This book has been organised to cover each of these units in detail. Headings are designed to make it easy to follow the content of each unit and to find the information needed to achieve a high grade. As well as providing information each unit is designed to stimulate the development of the thinking skills needed to achieve an advanced level award.

Assessment

Each unit will be assessed by coursework or by an external test set and marked by AQA. Detailed guidance for coursework assessment and external test requirements can be found in the unit specifications and at AQA's web site at www.aqa.org.uk. This book has been designed to support students to achieve high grades as set out in the guidance from AQA available during 2004/2005.

Special features of this book

Throughout the text there are a number of features that are designed to encourage reflection and to help students make links between theory

and practice. In particular this book has been designed to encourage a depth of learning and understanding and to encourage students to go beyond a surface level of descriptive writing.

The special features of this book include:

Think it over

The feature is designed to provide thought-provoking questions that will encourage reflective thinking, or possibly reflection involving discussion with others.

Did you know?

Interesting facts or snippets of information included to encourage reflective thinking.

Scenario

We have used this term in place of the more traditional term 'case study' because the idea of people being perceived as 'cases' does not fit easily with the notion of empowerment – a key value highlighted by government policy and by AQA standards. Scenarios are presented throughout the units to help explain the significance of theoretical ideas to Health, Social Care and Early Years settings.

Consider this

This feature appears at the end of each section and presents a brief scenario followed by a series of questions. These questions are designed to encourage reflection and analysis of the issues covered within the section.

Key concept

Because the authors believe that the development of analytic and evaluative skills requires the ability to use concepts, the authors have identified key concepts and offered a brief explanation of how these terms might be used.

Assessment guidance

At the end of each unit there is a 'how you will be assessed' section that provides either sample test material for externally assessed units or outline guidance and ideas designed to help students achieve the highest grades when preparing internally assessed coursework.

Glossary

This book contains a useful glossary to provide fast reference for key terms and concepts used within the units.

References

There is a full list of references used within each unit together with useful websites at the end of each unit.

Author details

Neil Moonie, former Deputy Director of the Department of Social Services, Health and Education in a College of Further and Higher Education. Chartered Psychologist, part-time lecturer and contributor to a wide range of textbooks and learning resources in the field of health and social care. Editor of Heinemann's GNVQ Intermediate and Advanced textbooks on health and social care since 1993 and editor of the 2000 Standards AVCE textbook.

Siân Lavers is a lecturer at a College of Further Education, teaching on the Levels Two and Three Health and Social Care Programmes, the BTEC National Diploma in Early Years and the CIEH Foundation Food Hygiene Certificate. She has contributed to several text books on Health and Social Care, S/NVQ 3 Care and Key Skills.

Dee Spencer-Perkins began her social services career in research, moving on to become a trainer and then a training manager. She is a Chartered Member of the Chartered Institute of Personnel and Development, and now works as an independent trainer, consultant and writer, and specialises in language and communication. Dee also has a keen interest in disability issues.

Beryl Stretch, former Head of Health and Social Care in a large College of Further Education. Currently part of the senior examining board for Edexcel, GCE and GCSE Health and Social Care. Former external and internal verifier for VCE, GNVQ, NVQ programmes and examiner for GCSE Human Biology. Contributor to several bestselling textbooks on health and social Care at all levels.

Acknowledgements

The authors and publisher would like to thank all those who have granted permission to reproduce copyright material.

The authors and publisher would like to thank the following for permission to reproduce photographs:

Alamy Images/archivberlin Fotoagentur GmbH/page 7
Alamy Images/Peter Titmuss/page 8
Richard Smith/page 12
Harcourt Education (UK schools)/page 29
Alamy Images/Photofusion Picture Library/page 38
Alamy Images/page 41
Science Photo LIbrary/ DR KARI LOUNATMAA/page 43
Richard Smith/page 44
Alamy Images/Janine Wiedel Photolibrary/page 45 (1)
Richard Smith/page 45 (2)
Richard Smith/page 50
Alamy Images/page 57
Harcourt Education/Jules Selmes/ page 68
Richard Smith/page 79
Getty Images/Stone/page 81
Harcourt Education/page 88
Corbis nrf/page 102
Harcourt Education/Jules Selmes/page 107 (1)
Photodisc/page 107 (2)
Corbis/page 108
Photodisc/page 111
Harcourt Education/ (UK Schools)/page 112
Harcourt Education/Tudor Photography (UK schools)/page 113
Alamy Images/Janine Wiedel Photolibrary/page 124
Science Photo Library/DR. E. WALKER/page 127
Science Photo Library/PARVIZ M. POUR/page 128

Every effort has been made to contact copyright holders of material produced in this book. Any omissions will be rectified in subsequent printings if notice is given to the publishers.

Effective caring

You will learn about:

1.1   Life quality factors
1.2   Treating people well
1.3   Caring skills and techniques
1.4   Services
1.5   Access to services
1.6   Rights and responsibilities of service users
1.7   Risks and safe working

Introduction

This unit introduces you to a selection of services which are provided for individuals in health and social care. It also covers factors that are necessary for a good quality of life and some of the skills and techniques which carers may use to ensure they treat service users well.

How you will be assessed

This unit is externally assessed through a written examination comprising four compulsory structured questions.

1.1 Life quality factors

There are many factors to take into account that enable people to enjoy a good quality of life. A common set of principles and values called the care value base was devised in 1992. The care value base is intended to provide guidelines for health and social care workers to ensure that the care they provide to service users is appropriate and takes into account individual needs and preferences.

There are three main areas of health and social care that are affected by the care value base. These are:

* fostering equality and diversity
* fostering people's rights and responsibilities
* maintaining confidentiality of information.

These can be further divided into five main elements:

* anti-discriminatory practice
* confidentiality
* individual rights
* personal beliefs and identity
* effective communication.

Psychological life quality factors

There are many factors that can affect a person's quality of life. Basic needs such as food and water, warmth and safety and security are physical factors, but psychological factors (including those shown in Figure 1.1) also play a large part in how people feel about their lives.

Occupation

Being occupied, or having something to do, whether it is paid work, volunteer work or taking part in a hobby or sporting activity, helps people to

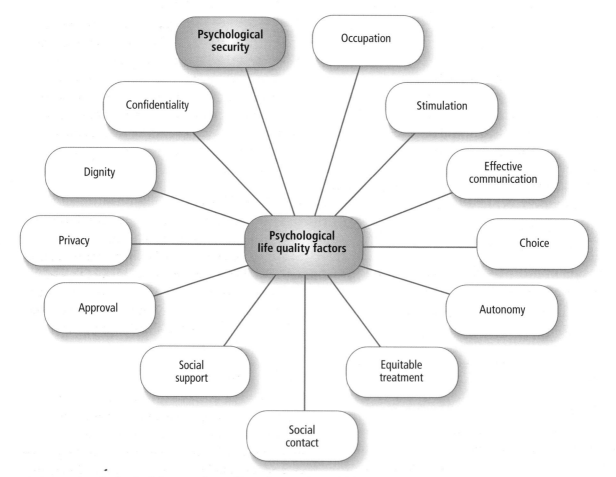

FIGURE 1.1 *Psychological factors that affect the quality of life*

feel that their existence is worthwhile. Certain activities provide people with status and this can be an important factor, as it helps to build self-confidence and self-esteem. Success at work or being the star player on a sports team will contribute to a general feeling of well-being, especially if what a person does is valued by others. This may also bring other benefits such as improving fitness levels or developing a wider social circle.

Stimulation

When people are stimulated by work or a particular interest, their minds are active and they feel challenged and motivated by what they are doing. Boredom can quickly set in when individuals feel that they have nothing to do, and this can develop into apathy – the less a person does, the less he or she wants to do, which can lead to depression. This can be a problem in some care settings, especially if a resident has previously lived a full and independent life. It is important to find out about an individual's interests and to try to provide appropriate stimulation for each service user.

Effective communication

Being able to communicate effectively provides many benefits. It allows for social contact and can help people to meet new friends by exchanging information. A carer who has good communication skills is able to provide information to service users, which can be used to improve their quality of life. This allows them to:

* find out, or be given information about their treatment, future opportunities or prospects

* be given coherent explanations for their condition and future treatment

* ask questions and receive answers

* be listened to.

All of these factors will help the service user to feel that their views and wishes are valued.

Choice

Having choice is linked to effective communication. Individuals only have choice when they know that there is more than one option to consider and make a decision about.

Choice provides a certain amount of power and a sense of freedom. Some choices may be quite minor such as being able to choose when, where and what you eat, but some are major decisions such as choosing a career or deciding whether or not to move house. For older people, a major decision may be about going into residential care. In order to make an informed choice the individual will need to know what options are available and practicalities such as cost, location and facilities. However, in some care settings service users may not have a great deal of choice in some matters.

Autonomy

Autonomy is the ability to have control over one's life and the opportunity to make one's own decisions. When people have the freedom to make choices about their life without being coerced, they are said to be autonomous.

Equitable treatment

This is the absence of unfair discrimination. In practice what it means is that a service user can receive treatment that is fair and not significantly better or worse than the treatment given to another person. Therefore, an individual, who because of his or her circumstances has a greater need than the individual in the next room, will receive that care regardless of the cost or resources needed.

Social contact

Social contact is the opportunity to be with other people. People who do not have any form of social contact can easily become isolated, which can lead to depression. Some people have a lot of social contact and are members of many different social groups, depending on their interests or work. This helps to develop a sense of self because such individuals have a sense of belonging.

Social support

This allows individuals to be provided with support from people whom they trust, such as friends and family. This can help to provide individuals with emotional security. Some people do not have family or many friends and may rely on social support from advocates or care workers.

Approval

When individuals know that their actions gain approval, affection or praise from others, they develop a sense of self-esteem.

Privacy

All service users have the right to privacy. This is particularly important if service users are receiving treatment that might be embarrassing, if they wish to be undisturbed, or if they wish to speak confidentially to a care worker. Maintaining privacy for service users shows respect for their wishes and can lead to a sense of trust developing between carers and service users.

Dignity

Being shown respect allows service users dignity. Providing care that does not demean individuals increases their self-esteem.

Confidentiality

The maintenance of confidentiality is a vital aspect of caring for others. Ensuring that sensitive information about a service user is not given to anyone who does not have the right to know it, helps to maintain an atmosphere of trust between carer and service user.

Psychological security

Psychological security means that individuals will not be afraid or anxious about any aspect of their life. Anyone who is facing a major life change may be worried about the consequences of the decisions they are making. Reassurance and effective communication can help to relieve any fears.

Physical life quality factors

A good quality of life can be influenced by factors that can be grouped together using the term 'physical life quality factors'. These include aspects of exercise, nutrition, safety, hygiene, comfort and being free from pain, as shown in Figure 1.2. For example, service users will feel that the caring they receive is not very effective if they are poorly fed and in pain.

Exercise

When we think of exercise, mental images of

Consider this

The Poplars is a large residential nursing and care home on the outskirts of a large town. Public transport links into the town centre are good and many staff and visitors use the bus on a daily basis. Although the rooms are clean and comfortable, few of the staff have any qualifications and only mandatory training such as moving and handling and fire training is provided. A new manager was appointed three days ago and she is shocked by the staff's lack of knowledge. Several incidents have been brought to her attention, which she feels must receive her immediate attention. Some of the incidents are listed below. Describe which psychological life quality factors are missing in these situations.

1. A visitor hears two of the care assistants talking on the bus. One says, 'I don't know how Mrs Smith has coped until now with looking after her husband, especially since she was diagnosed with breast cancer six months ago.'

2. Mrs Johnston's daughter arrives to visit and finds her sitting on a commode in her room with the door wide open.

3. Mr Brown was admitted to The Poplars a week ago and was told that the policy is that all service users are in bed by 8.30 pm. His favourite programme is on at 9.00 pm. He does not have a television in his room.

4. Mrs Davison is reluctant to receive care from Julia, the care assistant on duty. She calls her a nosy cow and tries to hit her.

gymnastic activity or school physical education tends to prevail in most people's minds. This is not necessarily what we mean when we consider exercise in terms of effective caring. However, this also does not mean that hydrotherapy, exercising in water and remedial gymnastics, for example, should be excluded in the overall consideration of exercise in this regard.

It has been known for a long time that adequate physical activity is crucially important both in society as a whole (see Unit 3.2 on page 107) and as part of daily living within the caring professional role.

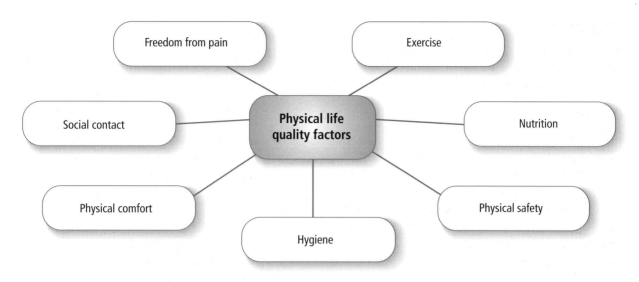

FIGURE 1.2 *Physical factors that affect the quality of life*

Infants need to exercise their limbs to promote sitting, crawling and walking. They love to be laid on a rug or blanket, without the encumbrance of a nappy, and kick their legs and wave their arms in sheer pleasure. Adding stimulation such as suspended toys and sound-making devices fills them with joy and promotes relaxation and sleep.

Infants may be given some time lying on their back and the front, and carers will often be surprised by how much an infant will change position even though there is as yet no strength in the limbs. This type of activity can start from only a few weeks old, as long as the infant is not left for too long and is content.

Later on, they should be given opportunities to support their weight on the legs and arms as in the crouch position, with their legs tucked up and arms bent at the elbow. An infant will soon let the carer know if it is unhappy. From 8–9 months of age onwards, under careful supervision, infants should be allowed to pull themselves up using a steady support such as heavy furniture; and this will promote walking at around age 13–15 months. Now and again, it is found that carers (usually paid) who are looking after more than one or two children will not encourage movement in these ways because a crawling and walking child needs more attention and vigilance. This is obviously something that needs to be given attention to and guarded against most carefully. Children also need fresh air, stimulation and short walks (carers may

find it useful to take the buggy on walks as well for when fatigue sets in). The carer should ensure that there is some form of restraint like a wrist strap or harness and reins because very young children have no sense of danger or road sense.

Children are more active than adults, but whether older children now get enough exercise to receive the full range of health benefits is unknown. We have learned (in a government paper) that 33 per cent of boys and around 40 per cent of girls undertake such low physical activity levels that in the future this may affect their health experience. (*At least five a week: evidence on the impact of physical activity and its relationship to health,* Chief Medical Officer of Health 2004).

Children at school should have at least one hour of moderately intense physical activity each day; and at least twice a week activities such as chasing games, skipping, running, jumping and gymnastics should be included to increase the density of bones and develop muscle strength.

> ✱ DID YOU KNOW?
>
> Currently, the only time that many children are intensely physically active occurs at school, and as play areas become less available and journeys to school are by bus or car, it is feared that this is far from adequate. Socio-economic factors also become important as leisure centre activity and team participation becomes expensive in time and money.

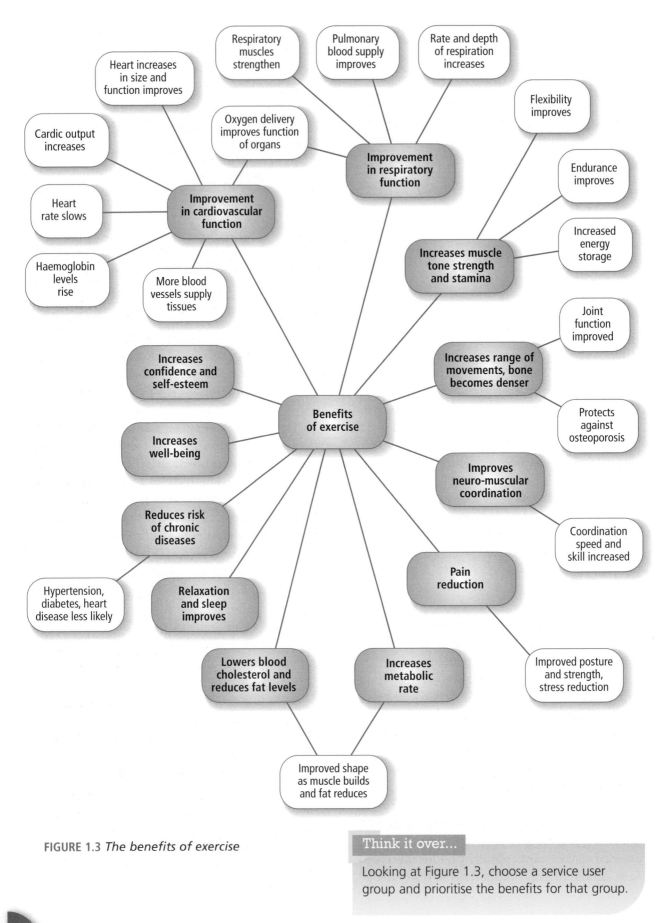

FIGURE 1.3 *The benefits of exercise*

Think it over...

Looking at Figure 1.3, choose a service user group and prioritise the benefits for that group.

Stuart is nearly seven years old; his parents saved enough money to send him and his brother to a football scheme in the summer holidays. He displayed a talent for football and was offered the opportunity to go to a football academy run by a premier league team in the area. Stuart is performing well and loves the sport, but training takes place a fair distance away on three nights of the week and often matches take place on Sundays. With three children in the family and two working parents without their own transport, life is becoming difficult. Stuart's 12-year-old sister gets bored watching Stuart play football and his brother also feels that he is not getting any attention. Stuart's parents feel that it is costing too much time and money to promote his sport and fear that they will soon be forced to give up the training. They are also worried about the effect on their other two children.

Competitive sports and other substantial ways of exercising are important sources of psychological well-being for most young adults and children, bringing improvements in mood, reduced tension and anxiety as well as social and emotional benefits. Young people with difficult, challenging and anti-social behaviour might change with a purposeful outlet for energy and emotion. Walking to school and cycling needs to be supported and encouraged with walking 'buses' and safer cycle paths.

Disabled people are now catered for in a way that has never happened before. There are workout videos and DVDs for people with developmental disabilities, multiple sclerosis, mental health problems, people recovering from heart attacks and strokes. Tai Chi, bowls, weight lifting, Bocce (Italian lawn bowling) and basketball are all prominent activities for those service users who have disabilities.

It seems that the only barrier to the creation of specialised exercise products is a lack of awareness. The Internet has proved to be a real asset for disabled service users in that it enables them to access products that are specific to their requirements. Some service users who require specialised physical activity sessions may attend physiotherapy departments in their local

hospitals and occupational therapists will also help in their rehabilitation. However, there are still plenty of opportunities to raise the quality of life for disabled people who have long been ignored.

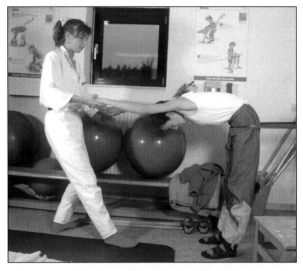

Exercising in a physiotherapy unit

People who sit or lie too long in one position may develop bed or pressure sores where the skin lies over a bone prominence; this happens because the body weight prevents the blood supply delivering oxygen and nutrients to the tissues. When the tissues break down because of inadequate blood supplies, the resulting sore can be difficult and

✳ DID YOU KNOW?

Carers and managers in the NHS are urged to participate and lead in developing sustainable and cost-effective physical activity strategies to meet health goals. We will expect to see more creative methods used to involve service users in physical activities including exercise referral initiatives, help and advice. Health care teams are to rethink their strategies on physical activity for those who are already suffering from chronic diseases such as osteoarthritis, depression, back pain, coronary heart disease and obesity.

For most adults, exercise that can be part of daily living is the easiest to accomplish – such as walking or cycling to work, or walking a few stops before getting on a bus, using stairs instead of lifts and taking up active hobbies or leisure pursuits.

slow to heal. Infection is a risk and major surgery may be required, as this can be life threatening.

Although aids such as sheepskins and foam cushions are useful to those suffering with bed or pressure sores, the priority for service users is to move and change position. Service users often need reminding to do this and encouraging their motivation is important. Wheelchair users are encouraged to lift themselves on their forearms from time to time to relieve the pressure.

> ✳ DID YOU KNOW?
>
> Over the last 25 years, walking and cycling have declined in England by 26 per cent and this in a period when public transport has been in decline. It is not surprising therefore that there are so many cars on the roads!

Physical activity slows the loss of bone mineral density in older adults; it may delay the progression of osteoarthritis and delay the onset of low back pain. It is also helpful to those people who have had joint replacements.

Housework is an excellent physical activity and wheelchair users and other service users can assist in this form of activity in residential accommodation. People in later adulthood clearly should be offered tasks commensurate with their abilities and capacities but at the same time should not sit in the same chair, day after day, watching television. An old adage used frequently in care is 'Use it or lose it'.

This is unfortunately very true, particularly with respect to mobility. Every time you perform a task for someone who could do it for him or herself, perhaps with difficulty or very slowly, you have moved that individual one step closer to dependency.

Some people, largely through ignorance, express dissatisfaction at seeing an older or disabled service user in care having to perform tasks for themselves. We must never be tempted to stop maintaining or increasing independence and mobility. Walking is the most important form of exercise and increasingly small goals must be incorporated into daily living. Mobility aids, patience, encouragement and support

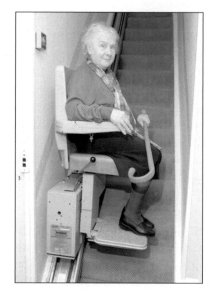

An older person being supported with mobility

must be part of physical activity for older service users.

One research study by Jirovek (1991) concluded that a daily exercise routine for older, mentally frail service users promoted greater mobility and continence. Many elderly service users deemed to have incontinence merely cannot get to the lavatory in time and using a commode chair to get there and walking back improves continence substantially.

The importance of assisting older service users to walk within their capabilities cannot be emphasised enough.

Nutrition

This is the process by which an individual takes in and uses food. As well as eating to survive and being aware of the current interest in the relationship between food and physical health, it is important to remember that food forms a major part of social and cultural living. A carer must help in promoting a pleasant social environment for service users when they are eating. The dining area should be cheerful with tablecloths, napkins, place mats and condiments, as eating food in well-organised surroundings helps to stimulate the appetite and foster good table manners.

Service users should choose their own food from a menu with assistance, where necessary, to promote preferences and any special dietary needs. This will include cultural, ethnic and religious requirements when appropriate.

Fasting is also important in certain religious festivals and carers need to be aware that urging some service users to participate in mealtimes may offend them.

It is also worth remembering that important life events, such as christenings, weddings and funerals, are usually celebrated by sharing food. Service users in care may miss these events and be disinclined to participate in normal meals.

✱ DID YOU KNOW?

The World Health Organisation (Jan. 2005) has carried out a massive six-year study of babies in several continents, who are breast-fed and born to non-smoking mothers, with startling results. Growth charts used to measure progress were largely based on babies fed on formula milk (bottle-fed babies) and are wrong. Babies who are breast-fed are lighter by around 7 per cent than formula-fed babies. In fact, some babies thought to be underweight were transferred to formula milk in an attempt to put on weight. Many babies were probably not underweight, and in fact the bonny, bouncing formula babies are overweight and even in some cases obese. This has serious implications, as the rate of weight gain in childhood is reckoned to be a key determinant of whether teenagers and adults suffer from obesity, heart disease and Type II diabetes in later life. There is now an urgent need for the international growth charts to be rewritten.

You will find more information on nutrition and malnutrition in Unit 3 on page 104.

Babies and toddlers who do not grow at an expected rate are said to fail to thrive.

Under-nourishment may arise from home problems such as a poor relationship between mother and child or even neglect. Delayed social, emotional and intellectual skills as well as poor growth, tend to occur in deprived children. There is a possibility that a child in a stable family who is receiving adequate nutrition yet fails to thrive may be suffering from serious physical disorders.

Several studies comparing dietary intake and growth have concluded that the quality and quantity of food intake declines with poverty. In poor families, where genetic factors can be discounted, the oldest child tends to be taller than younger siblings and a possible explanation is that the larger the family the smaller the quantity of shared food. Many mothers will go without food so that their children will eat. In Britain, there are still families in poverty suffering from malnourishment but so, too, are some affluent families, not from lack of food but the wrong type of food. Malnutrition arises when any component of food is taken in incorrect quantities. Too much fat, salt and sugar in the diet, very often from convenience foods, can lead to obesity, see Unit 3, page 104.

With all life stages, input should equal output – that is to say that the amount of food taken in must equal the amount of energy expended. With an increasingly sedentary population, input is tending to vastly exceed output, resulting in an overweight or obese population with long-term effects.

Adults need to vary their food habits in accordance with their lifestyles. With the decline of heavy agricultural labour and the mining and manufacturing industries, together with the increase of electronic and service industries, the myth that a working man needs a hearty meal when he comes home from work is no longer valid for most families. The meal portions in care establishments are a frequent source of complaint and service users often supplement the food provided with food gifts from visitors and family. Although public service meals are provided to a restricted budget, service users are clearly used to a larger quantity of food. Food habits are hard to give up and at home, meal providers tend to serve the same portions regardless of changes in circumstances.

Ill people and those with poor appetites, in particular, need to have food presented in an attractive way and not be over-faced with large quantities. Food should have a pleasant smell and taste, as well as appearance. Some people may be on special diets, such as patients who suffer from coeliac disease, renal failure and phenylketonuria; it is easy to become disaffected with a diet in these circumstances and service users may consume outlawed food or become disinterested in food as a result.

Carers need to be well informed about nutritional needs, as some service users may enter a caring establishment with lifelong eating habits that are less than healthy. However, common sense needs to prevail; if service users have reached later adulthood, despite 'unhealthy' diets, perhaps high in fat, salt and sugar, they may be deprived of important calories and fat-soluble vitamins (Vitamins A, D, E and K) with enforced change, and they certainly would not feel very happy. Elderly service users may have lost some sense of smell and/or taste; they may have problems with swallowing and either poorly fitting or a complete lack of teeth, leading ultimately to problems with nutrition.

Service users entering residential care frequently do so because they have been unable to care for themselves in the recent past. Consequently, such service users may have forgotten to eat for long periods or eat bizarre combinations of food. Such difficulties will usually clear up in a few weeks but special requirements such as extra protein and vitamins may be required temporarily.

Individuals who have suffered a stroke may need food cut up in small pieces and special cutlery aids to assist with nutrition. Visually impaired service users may require food to be placed in particular plate locations and others may require fluids to drink to help with swallowing drier foods. All elderly service users should be encouraged to drink plenty of fluids;

they tend to restrict their fluid intake if they are anxious about incontinence.

Physical safety and hygiene

The key word here is probably vigilance; a carer must always be alert for risks and hazards. When you are caring for an individual or group of service users you cannot let any harm befall them. Service users would not be in care unless they were in need of someone to look after them. They may be too young, in later adulthood, disabled, ill or infirm service users.

There must be safe limits for infants' and toddlers' activities and safe toys for them to play with. Suitable precautions should be taken to guard against infection and any child who has an infection cared for with minimal risk to others. Sometimes this is difficult, as many infections have long incubation periods and children can pass on the disease before adults are aware of its existence. In this case, parents and guardians must be made aware of the possibility of an infection being spread.

Crockery and utensils must be washed well in hot water and detergent and babies' feeding bottles must be sterilised. Waste materials such as dirty nappies must be bagged and disposed of safely and all spills cleared up immediately. Some minor accidents and tumbles will inevitably occur because youngsters are by nature inquisitive and adventurous; parents need to be informed so that they, in turn, can keep a watchful eye on their children at home.

It is not sufficient to notice hazards, you must deal with them properly and promptly or make the area as safe as possible by using warning signs, closing down or closing off the hazard, and reporting it immediately to a supervisor. You should use common sense regarding the hazards you can manage and those you cannot do anything about due to your own lack of knowledge and expertise.

For example, you can mop up spilt water, remove furniture from corridors or pick up fallen objects, but do not try to repair broken equipment or deal with hazardous materials unless you have had special training. You should pay particular attention to trailing electrical flexes, worn furnishings and floor coverings, broken or faulty equipment, slippery floors and any obstructions to exits and fire escapes.

Just as you would do in your own home, challenge and check out everyone you meet who you are not familiar with. Do not assume that because visitors are wearing some type of uniform on, they are bona fides – this is the most common way for people who are 'up to no good' to gain access into care establishments that are usually not locked. Ask for proof of identity. Nowadays, most organisations provide identity badges or cards, and it may be necessary to call the organisation that the individual claims to be representing to check on authenticity. Many old people have been 'conned' by criminals, who state that they are from the council, utility services or similar, and have suffered greatly as a result.

Elderly people are vulnerable because they are too trusting. Often they come from communities where doors were left unlocked so that neighbours could come and go.

Some service users may have valuable property that should be safeguarded; such items should be placed in safety and a record kept that includes a description of each one. Supervisors should be aware of any service users who keep large sums of money or valuables so that they may be made aware of the risks and responsibilities associated with refusing to use the facilities for safekeeping.

You also need to guard against aggressive or violent people; these may be visitors or service users (and sometimes carers themselves). Ensure that you are not alone, be close to an exit door and/or emergency alarm and never give out information that you are not permitted to give.

It is not advisable to lift service users manually or use lifting equipment unless a qualified person has trained you. You may permanently damage yourself, colleagues or service users.

It is essential that carers of all service users, not just infants and children, ensure that they always wash their hands carefully, particularly before and after:

* preparing and handling food
* assisting with the toilet
* assisting with personal hygiene
* disposing of any waste material such as nappies, bedpans and urine bottles
* any medical procedure
* touching animals, pets
* cleaning
* touching any contaminated material.

Think it over...

There are several important legislative documents that you need to be aware of, as well as organisational policies in workplaces. Some of the most important are:

* Health and Safety at Work Act 1974 (HASAWA)
* Control of Substances Hazardous to Health 1988 (COSHH)
* Reporting of Injuries, Diseases and Dangerous Occurrences Regulations (1985) (RIDDOR)
* Manual Handling Regulations (1992)
* Health and Safety First Aid Regulations (1981)
* Management of Health and Safety at Work Regulations (1992)

Most organisations have fire safety procedures and require all staff to attend fire lectures. Make sure that you are familiar with the requirements of the organisation.

* DID YOU KNOW?

There are three types of hand washing:

* social – using soap and water
* antiseptic – using an antiseptic detergent solution or alcohol rub
* surgical – washing with an antiseptic detergent for at least 3 minutes.

Poor hand cleansing and faulty technique continues to cause the spread of infection via hands. Service users may also be to blame. In a study made by Pritchard and Hathaway (1988) of 20 male service users, 60 per cent did not wash their hands after using the toilet. Of those who could walk to the toilet themselves, 50 per cent did not wash their hands and none of those who could not walk did. In the majority of these cases, the carer did not offer to help the service users to wash their hands.

Carers frequently report washing their hands more often than they are observed to do. In many cases, the hands are not washed very carefully; the areas between the fingers are usually poorly cleaned, and the thumb, palm creases and tips of the middle and ring fingers are often not carefully washed. If carers themselves do not wash their hands carefully or provide advice to service users, particularly children, infection will continue to be spread in this way.

Hand washing

There has been a lot of bad publicity about the lack of clean hospitals and the rising number of cases of MRSA infection, resulting in serious damage to people's health and a significant number of deaths. The media attention has caused the government some considerable embarrassment and resulted in a number of changes in the way hospitals are cleaned. This is a wake-up call for all care establishments that physical safety and cleanliness are of paramount importance in ensuring that the health of service users is not put at risk through shoddy work and bad practice. Kitchen and food hygiene must be included in this too; there have been numerous reports of food poisoning cases from hospitals, residential establishments, nurseries and schools in the past. In some cases, deaths of infants and older people have occurred, as these are the most vulnerable groups for food poisoning illness.

Make a list of the most important hygiene recommendations for food handling and kitchen working to refresh your mind. You will find Food Hygiene and Food Handling qualifications informative and useful.

Physical comfort

Infants and young children who cannot express themselves verbally may cry when uncomfortable with pain, dirty nappies, stickiness or dirt; but it is subject to individual emotion and experience. Some children never seem to mind and others get distressed easily. Lack of emotion is no excuse for not dealing with a situation that can lead to skin complaints and infections.

Children who are articulate will say when they are uncomfortable and so will adults.

A service user who cannot get adequate rest, relaxation or sleep may become irritable, depressed and bad-tempered. Mental activities become less accurate and medication omitted or mistaken. Different people require different periods of sleep and some people like to stay up into the small hours of the morning and sleep until noon, while others are up early and ready to go to bed around 10.00 or 11.00 pm.

Have you ever experienced 'jet-lag'? When your own sleep patterns have been disturbed it can take 2 or 3 days to feel as though you are 'back to normal'.

FIGURE 1.4 *Hospital is often not a restful place*

Many people complain of being unable to rest during a stay in hospital; there are others around you, lights on, people talking quietly, the telephone rings constantly, the bed and bedding feels different and cleaners arrive early in the morning (see Figure 1.4). Service users often say that they need to go home to get a rest!

Some things you can do to make a service user comfortable at night:

✳ provide physical and mental exercise during the day

✳ make sure that the room is not too cold or too hot

✳ use the lavatory before getting into bed

✳ relieve anxieties as much as possible

✳ warm, preferably milky drink before bed-time

✳ keep noise and light down to a minimum

✳ make bed comfortable with support pillows as necessary

✳ avoid stimulants such as caffeine, spicy food and alcohol late in the evening.

A quiet, resting period should also be scheduled into daylight hours and many establishments will have their own strategy for this. Open visiting can be a problem. Visitors who arrive just as service users are settling down, for example, may not be aware of the disturbance they cause; this may present the opportunity for a carer to suggest a slightly earlier or later time for visiting.

Service users should be able to choose their own clothing for comfort although a carer can make helpful suggestions.

It is important when lifting and moving service users to discuss what you are going to do, obtain consent and talk about how they can assist and cooperate. A service user must not be treated like a carcass of meat that is moved from one place to another and must be comfortable with the procedure.

Freedom from pain

Management of pain is an important part of caring for someone, but you may not always know about the pain. Some people can bear strong pain and others cannot bear slight pain; it is a very personal experience comprising both physical and emotional factors. You should be aware of the need to ask if a service user is in pain if they are unusually quiet, distressed, tense, fidgeting or sweating. Some service users will put up with the pain for quite some time, as they do not want to bother people, other service users are frightened of pain and will tell you straight away. It is also important to be aware of the difficulties that might be faced in expressing symptoms of pain by people with learning disabilities, speech and hearing problems and those who do not have English as their first language.

Always listen sympathetically to service users who complain of pain and ask whether you can assist them in some way. When someone is used to a particular type of pain, they may have a remedy that works for them such as curling up with a hot-water bottle or taking two Paracetamol tablets. Always refer the service user to a supervisor and check that it is all right to manage the pain as the service user wishes. Sometimes, if an investigation is being carried out, pain relief might be withheld so that the medical team can assess the situation accurately. On other occasions, particularly with an accident or injury, there might be the possibility of a surgical operation and it would be dangerous to provide medication, however simple.

Sometimes a service user in pain can be helped by moving into a better position, massaging the area affected or by the application of warmth or cold (ice pack). Chronic muscular pain can be helped by a TENS machine (transcutaneous electrical nerve stimulation) and the service user can walk about while this is happening.

Walking about and talking to others helps some people, while others like a warm bath or carrying out a task to take the mind off the pain.

There are several 'alternative therapies' that many service users rely upon, such as acupuncture, reflexology, meditation, yoga and aromatherapy. These should be part of the total care package and should be openly discussed with the medical team.

There are also various medications that provide pain relief such as Aspirin, Codeine, Paracetamol, combinations of these, Ibruprofen and morphine derivatives. Qualified, experienced carers only should administer these drugs.

Think it over...

Research one alternative therapy and evaluate its effectiveness in the management of pain.

1.2 Treating people well

You have just learned what life quality factors are. The term 'treating people well' means providing life quality factors that match the needs and personality of the individual. An example of this would be to ensure that any individual who is capable of expressing a preference should be offered choice, such as what to eat at mealtimes. Every individual is different and should be treated with equality. This does not, however, mean treating everyone the same.

There are ethical and practical reasons why people should be treated well. Care workers who provide care for others have an ethical duty to ensure that the care they provide safeguards the interests of the individuals and maintains as good a quality of life as possible.

In practical terms, treating people well leads to a good working relationship which is based on trust. If service users are treated well they trust those providing the care and behave cooperatively. If carers are treated with respect by those for whom they are providing care, they will make sure that they do the same in return.

There are many ways in which people can be treated badly, which has a negative effect on their self-esteem and self-confidence.

Ways in which people can be treated badly

Neglect

Neglect means to leave someone uncared for. In a care setting this could mean not meeting physical needs such as, for example, failing to provide care in helping individuals to use the lavatory, washing or feeding them. Neglect could also involve not meeting psychological needs such as communication or safety and security. Any of these could lead to an individual feeling unvalued and will create feelings of low self-esteem. It may also lead to a feeling of fear and insecurity. In a home care setting where the main carer may be a relative with little or no experience, an individual may be neglected because of a lack of knowledge, rather than a deliberate act of cruelty.

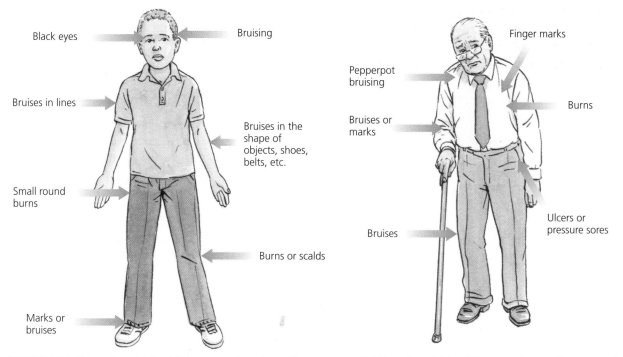

Black eyes

Bruising

Bruises in lines

Bruises in the shape of objects, shoes, belts, etc.

Small round burns

Burns or scalds

Marks or bruises

Finger marks

Pepperpot bruising

Burns

Bruises or marks

Bruises

Ulcers or pressure sores

FIGURE 1.5A *Ways in which children can be abused*

B *Ways in which older people can be abused*

> The Department of Health (1999: 5) defines child neglect as:
>
> *'the persistent failure to meet a child's basic physical and/or psychological needs, likely to result in the serious impairment of the child's health or development. It may involve a parent or carer failing to provide adequate food, shelter and clothing, failing to protect a child from physical harm or danger, or the failure to ensure access to appropriate medical care or treatment. It may also include neglect of, or unresponsiveness to, a child's basic emotional needs'.*
>
> Source: www.nspcc.org.uk/inform

✳ DID YOU KNOW?

Since its launch in 1986, the charity Childline has counselled over one million children and young people.

Over 1,000 volunteers provide a 24-hour helpline for children in distress or danger. There are eleven counselling centres in the United Kingdom and about 4,000 children call Childline every day but only about 2,300 will get through due to lack of funds.

Rejection

Rejection of someone means not accepting them. Reasons for rejecting people may be based on unacceptable behaviour or their not conforming to recognised norms and values. New mothers who suffer from post-natal depression can reject their babies and this can cause long-term relationship problems between them and their child if they are not offered support.

Hostility

A carer who is hostile to a service user will be unable to create a good working relationship with that individual. Hostility may be due to a lack of understanding about the individual or a fundamental disagreement regarding his or her beliefs and values. Of course, it is also possible for a service user to be hostile towards a care worker, especially if the individual feels that his or her way of life is being threatened.

Punishment

Punishment is the application of sanctions against someone if it is believed that they have committed an act which is not acceptable. It is never acceptable for a carer to punish a service user for a real or imagined misdemeanour, especially if the individual is already in a vulnerable position which might result in fear. A carer must always remember that they may find themselves in a position of power and this must never be abused.

Bullying

Bullying is defined as deliberately hurtful behaviour, repeated over a period of time.

The Andrea Adams Trust defines bullying as:

✳ unwarranted, humiliating, offensive behaviour towards an individual or groups of employees

✳ persistently negative malicious attacks on personal or professional performance which are typically unpredictable, unfair, irrational and often unseen

✳ an abuse of power or position that can cause such anxiety that people gradually lose all belief in themselves, suffering physical ill health and mental distress as a direct result

✳ the use of position or power to coerce others by fear or persecution, or to oppress them by force or threat.

Source www.channel4.com/health

The above definitions relate to bullying in the workplace, but can just as easily apply to care settings. It is not only service users who might be bullied. They might bully staff, or staff might bully other staff. In any of these cases, a difficult working environment may result and can severely affect an individual's self-esteem and self-confidence.

Violence

Violence is never acceptable in care settings. Notwithstanding the very real danger of physical harm being done to someone, the fear of harm can lead to withdrawal and depression. It might cause individuals to behave in a way that is quite different to their normal pattern of behaviour and this might be the first sign to a care worker that there is a problem.

Unfair discrimination

Unfair discrimination can occur on the basis of gender, sexuality, ethnicity, religion, social class, age and impairment. None of these are acceptable in a care environment and there are Acts of Parliament such as the Sex Discrimination Act 1975, the Disability Discrimination Act 1995 and the Race Relations Act 1976 which are in place to ensure equality for everyone. People who are discriminated against may not receive the care and support that they need and will feel unvalued. This is another aspect of bad treatment that will affect people's self-esteem and self-confidence.

Summary

This section has provided an overview of factors that can result in people being treated badly. All are unacceptable but this is especially the case in care work. The negative consequences are very far-reaching and an older vulnerable person may never fully recover from the effects.

Consider this

The Patterson family all live in the same street in a rather rundown area. Joe and Mandy are 28 and 26 years old and have four children, Josh aged nine, Jenny aged seven and twins Julie and James aged five. Two doors away are James senior and Peggy, Joe's parents who look after Betty, Peggy's mother who is 82 years old. Betty has been widowed for 15 years and has become increasingly frail. Her hearing and sight are both poor and she is waiting for a cataract operation. She is also in the early stages of Alzheimer's disease. Peggy is Betty's main carer, but she also looks after the children after school from 3.00 pm until 5.30 pm when Mandy finishes work at the local shoe shop. Joe works shifts and alternates weekly between 8.00 am to 5.00 pm and 3.00 pm to 11.00 pm. Money is tight for both households and Peggy often feels under great pressure. She is worried about how she will cope as Betty's condition deteriorates.

One day Sheila, the district nurse, makes a routine home visit to Betty to see how she is. She takes Betty's blood pressure and notices that she has bruises on her upper arms. She appears distressed and tearful. When she is unable to say how they happened, Sheila asks Peggy. Betty immediately becomes defensive and denies all knowledge of the bruises. When pressed, Peggy becomes verbally abusive and orders Sheila out of the house.

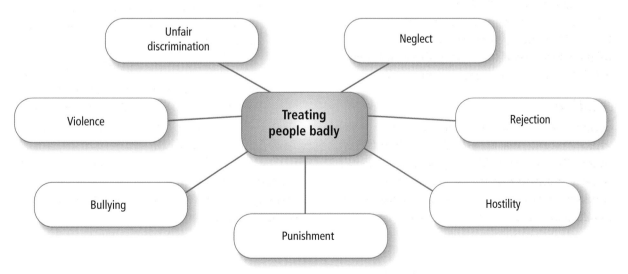

FIGURE 1.6 *Some of the ways in which people may be treated badly*

Mandy has recently noticed that Jenny is very quiet and withdrawn. When she tries to ask her what is wrong, she says that she is fine. Mandy has noticed that two of the Christmas presents she saved hard to buy her are nowhere in the house. Jenny is unable to provide an explanation for their disappearance. Josh has mentioned that he does not think that Jenny is very happy at school and does not appear to have any friends, but is unwilling or unable to say more.

1. Which individuals do you think might be being treated badly, in what way and who by?

2. What suggestions do you think Sheila could make to overcome some of the problems that have resulted in some members of the family being treated badly?

3. Which other professionals could be involved in helping the family to resolve their problems?

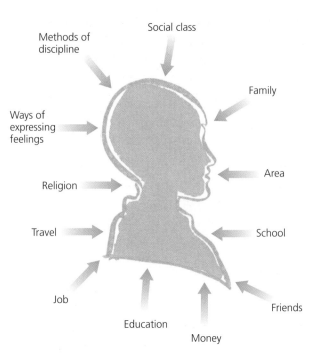

FIGURE 1.7 *People differ in their attitudes to others*

Barriers to treating people well – attitudes and prejudices

There can be different barriers that can cause difficulties when trying to treat people well. These can include:

* barriers internal to carers
* service user barriers.

Barriers internal to carers

Attitudes and prejudices

Barriers can arise when carers have attitudes and prejudices that do not coincide with those of service users. Prejudice involves the use of stereotypes to try to explain or categorise particular groups in society. A carer's background and upbringing will help to develop beliefs, values and norms that might not be the same as some of the individuals that they are employed to look after. Attitudes and prejudices that people hold can often have been an influence since an early age. For example, if someone is brought up from an early age to believe that black or Asian people are inferior to white people, then when

older, that individual might value them less and provide an inferior level of care. It is important that carers are aware of their background and beliefs and use this in a positive way to provide the best possible care to service users.

> **Think it over...**
>
> An important part of being an effective carer is being able to reflect on your practice and think about how you behave towards others and why. Think about the situations you have observed at your work experience placement. Do the care workers treat some service users differently than others? In what way is the treatment different? What do you think might be the reasons for this? Use Figure 1.6 to help you to identify some of the factors you might have come across.

Stereotyping

Stereotyping is using a range of characteristics or labels to describe a person or a group of people. This type of labelling is often negative and unfair; for example, a person who is overweight might be perceived as lazy and slow, or a young black man may be seen as being a drug-using criminal. However, every person is an individual and will have different characteristics, both positive and negative. Stereotyping may lead to discrimination, as a person's perception about a group of people, whether it is gender, sexuality, social class or race, will influence how that individual interacts with them. Although stereotyping can be an easy way of categorising people and making sense of the world, it is important to remember that all people are individual and unique, with individual and unique needs which must be met.

Lack of motivation

One of the keys to good team work is to ensure that all the members of the team are motivated. Having a set purpose and clear goals that everyone works towards will provide the 'glue' that holds the team together. In addition, individual motivation of team members will depend on each person having the opportunity to have his or her needs met, whether this is through training or taking on particular responsibilities that the individual is interested in.

Lack of motivation can arise when there is no common purpose and care workers become disenchanted or demoralised with the work they are doing. This may lead to a reduction in the quality of care that is provided to service users, and service users who become aware of this may feel that they are not sufficiently valued.

One of the ways in which motivation can be maintained is to ensure that there are sufficient

challenges for the team that will allow everyone to remain motivated and keep morale high. Setting challenges that will improve the quality of the care being offered will give service users a sense of well-being and value.

Conformity with inappropriate workplace norms

When a child starts school or an individual begins a new job, they become socialised into the norms of the establishment that they have joined. This means that they will learn the rules and routines that are considered to be normal and acceptable modes of behaviour. Some care workers can have negative experiences if they have worked in a care setting that does not pay sufficient attention to the types of behaviour that are acceptable. An example of this would be communicating in a way with service users and colleagues that might be seen as rude or lacking in respect. This may involve verbal or non-verbal communication, and inappropriate physical contact can make a service user feel very uncomfortable.

Pre-occupation with own needs

Sometimes staff can become pre-occupied with their own needs and fail to put the needs of their service users first. An example of this would be a situation in which a care assistant who is due to go off duty in five minutes is asked by a service user to be helped to the toilet. The care assistant says that she is going off duty in five minutes and will ask another member of staff to help her. However, she forgets to do so and half an hour later another care assistant goes to see the resident and finds her very distressed as she has wet herself. Putting her own needs first resulted in a very distressing situation for her service user, and although the care assistant has the right to get off duty on time, she also has a responsibility to ensure that all her service users receive appropriate care promptly, and she should have remembered to communicate her service user's need to another member of staff before leaving. Although it can be difficult to put aside one's own needs and wishes, care workers must always be aware that the needs of service users must take priority over their own needs.

Think it over...

Think about the activities you do now or have done in the past. This could be school work or further study, hobbies or sport. Were your activities carried out alone or as part of a team? Think about how you feel or felt about each of the activities you undertake now or undertook in the past. Do you think that your level of motivation influenced how successful you were, and did working alone or as part of a team influence your motivation? Can you think of reasons for your answers?

Lack of skill

Lack of skill can occur for a variety of reasons. It can occur as a result of inexperience, lack of training or an inability to reach the level of skill that is required of an effective care worker. Carers have a responsibility to identify their training needs and ask their manager to meet these needs. Senior carers and managers also have a responsibility to ensure that all mandatory training is provided, such as fire and manual handling training, and they should also identify any other training needs that are considered necessary for staff to carry out their duties in a proper manner.

Although it can be difficult for a carer to accept that they do not have the skills necessary to provide the level of care that is needed by some individuals, it can sometimes be kinder for a manager to point this out. If there is little appreciable sign of improvement after a set amount of time and considerable attempts to provide training, it might be appropriate to encourage a carer who is lacking some or all of the above skills to consider an alternative career. Managers do have a responsibility to ensure that the carers they employ have the skills and knowledge to provide high-quality care to service users, and they must be confident of this.

Service user barriers

Lack of status and power

There are different groups in society who are perceived or perceive themselves as being less valuable than others. These can be people with disabilities, older people or people with mental health problems. Status helps people to define how people are treated by others and how they see themselves. It is linked to the roles people have, and if an individual feels that he or she does not have a defined role, then they may also feel that they have little or no status in society.

There are cultural differences in the way that different groups of people are accorded status. In China, high status is awarded to the elder members of a family because they are seen by the other members as having wisdom and experience. In the United Kingdom, there is less respect shown to older people and they are seen as being needy and dependent. This can lead to feelings of insecurity and low self-esteem. It can be a confusing time for an older person who is no longer able to care for him or herself at home and has to enter residential care. Such individuals may feel that any status or power that they had in their working life has disappeared, and may put up barriers that make them resistant to receiving care from others.

It is very important for care professionals to make sure that they use good communication skills with their service users, so gaining a lot of information about them including their likes and dislikes; this will enable the carers to ensure that service users' needs can be met and they can be provided with choice and the opportunity to maintain some of the interests they had before entering residential care. This will in turn help to maintain their self-esteem and self-confidence, and gradually any barriers can be broken down.

Concealing real needs

Many service users will conceal what their real needs or worries are because they do not want to be a nuisance to those who look after them. Other reasons for concealing their real needs might be embarrassment if they find it difficult to talk about intimate problems. This may especially be the case for older ladies who might feel very uncomfortable discussing such subjects, especially if they may have to do so with a young male doctor or carer. Often, an individual will present with an entirely different problem and it will depend upon the skills of the carer to identify whether there is a greater problem that they are reluctant to talk about.

Tendency to exaggerate

Some service users will exaggerate their illness, needs or concerns in order to guarantee appropriate care. Sometimes this will be an attention-seeking device if an individual is lonely and feels in need of care or social contact. Although an individual may exaggerate, it is important that care workers do not trivialise their concerns, which may be very real to the individual concerned.

Hostile or obstructive behaviour

Sometimes individuals will display hostile or obstructive behaviour to carers or to other service users. This may be due to a medical condition such as dementia, or to fear about what is happening to them. Service uses may lash out as a form of defence or because they are frustrated at not being able to voice their concerns in a way that can be understood. Behaviour can be obstructive if a person is denying that they have a problem and need support. Under no circumstances should carers put themselves at risk if service users become violent when attempting to resist the provision of care. It is never worth putting oneself at risk. In such a situation the carer should immediately consult with a senior member of staff to discuss whether alternatives could or should be offered.

Summary

This section has looked at how to treat people well and the barriers that might arise that might prevent such treatment. It is important to remember that all elements of the care value base must be taken into account to ensure the good treatment of service users.

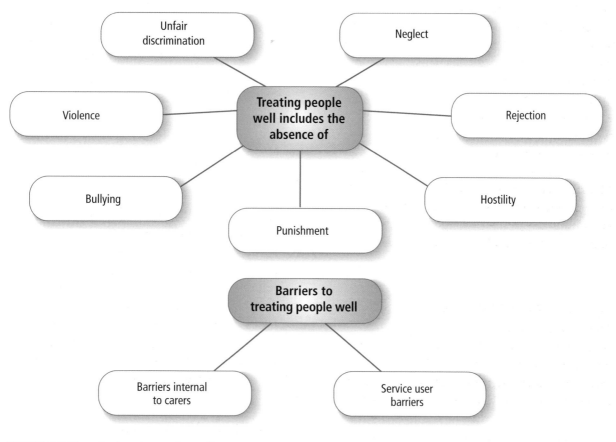

FIGURE 1.8 *How to treat people well*

Mary has just started work in a residential home for adults with learning difficulties. Sarah, one of the senior carers, has been asked to spend the shift with her showing her round the home and introducing her to the service users. During the tour, Mary starts to become a little worried about what she is seeing. Several of the residents look dirty and unkempt and one or two are sitting alone in their rooms with apparently nothing to do. Mary notices that one of them is blind. Another resident is displaying aggressive behaviour to others in the television room and two members of staff are attempting to restrain him. They are shouting at him and telling him that he is being very naughty.

In the dining room two of the carers are having their coffee and smoking in front of residents. Even though one of the residents is asking them to play a board game, the staff just say, 'Go away, Joe, we're having coffee – we need a break from you sometimes, you know.'

As they complete their tour of the home, Mary says to Sarah that she is surprised at the disrespectful way that the carers speak to the residents, and that she has noticed that some of the residents seem withdrawn and a little afraid of the staff. Sarah replies that it's just teasing and a bit of a laugh and that none of the residents have complained about the way they are spoken to, and in any case they're all 'retarded and don't notice'.

1. What factors can you identify that might indicate that the residents are not being treated well?

2. Why is this behaviour from the staff unacceptable?

3. Why might the residents be afraid of the staff?

4. What do you think Mary should do?

5. What do you think the management should do?

1.3 Caring skills and techniques

Promoting the optimal environment for supporting service users

Carers develop special skills and techniques in order to promote the optimal environment for supporting service users and making a difference to their health and daily activities. These abilities come with training and practice and need to form part of every carer's self-assessment and reflection cycle. It is useful to keep notes on the outcomes of practice and to consider how techniques can be improved.

> **Key concept**
>
> *Social perception* is the ability to recognise accurately how service users are feeling, their needs and intentions.

Perception

Perceptions can be accurate and inaccurate and we must be aware of making assumptions that are wrong. Prejudices arise from assumptions and we must guard against falling into the trap of discrimination and stereotyping. It is commonly recognised that the verbal component of a one-to-one conversation is less than 35 per cent and mostly information-giving while over 65 per cent is non-verbal and provides all manner of clues about a variety of subjects. A good carer is intuitive and can pick up and receive non-verbal signals that may actually be in conflict with the spoken words.

To communicate effectively, there must be eye-to-eye contact; we are all familiar with an individual who finds it uncomfortable to meet one's gaze. In Western culture this is taken to mean that the person is keeping information back or being less than truthful. We must be aware of different cultures, however, because in Japan, for instance, most people gaze at the neck rather than the face because it is considered to be offensive. Conversely, people who hold your gaze for a considerable length of time are interested in you or

hostile towards you. The size of the pupils of the eye provides the clue; dilated pupils signify interest whereas negative, aggressive feelings constrict the pupils. You need to practice interpreting signs such as these.

Service users, for example, may put up barriers towards you by crossing their arms and/or legs (known as a closed position); in doing so they demonstrate that they may be defensive and are withdrawing from the conversation. An open position with legs slightly apart and arms relaxed, often with the palms uppermost, may be associated with an honest and truthful display (see Figure 1.9).

Service users who pick imaginary fluff from their clothes while looking towards the floor are showing a very common sign of disapproval with the content of the communication, and those who pick at their cuffs, buttons and watches may be displaying nervousness. Service users who are anxious will rarely have their hands open; it is far more likely that they will have a closed fist that shows white knuckles. Even though the words used indicate that the service users are not worried, the behaviour described here and biting the lips would indicate otherwise. Anxious people may look paler than usual, be more distracted and seem quieter than usual.

Service users who feel 'down' or depressed frequently have their head bent down and eyes on the floor; their gait is more shuffling and they take smaller steps, their clothing tends to be coloured grey, brown or black and they make little effort to look nice.

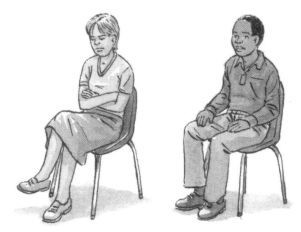

FIGURE 1.9 *Body posture can indicate attitude to others*

Observation

Observation is rather like the Advanced Motoring Test, where the examiner expects you to be aware of your surroundings for quite some distance ahead and behind you, regardless of whether it forms an immediate threat or not. You are expected to be pro-active in any given situation rather than retro-active. Being pro-active means that you are anticipating or thinking ahead about what might happen and the potential response is already forming; to be retro-active, on the other hand, means responding to a situation that has already happened.

Once again, skills like these need practice and reflection and then consideration about whether action should be taken. You might ask yourself questions similar to the following while you are carrying out your normal daily work tasks:

* Were any service users acting differently?

* Were any service users particularly drowsy or alert?

* Did the appetites of service users change?

* Did physical measurements of body temperature or blood pressure vary more than usual?

* Can I account for noticeable changes?

* How long have these changes been apparent?

* Do I need to record the changes, refer to colleagues or respond to the variation?

* At what time intervals do I need to repeat my observations?

* Am I missing something important?

* Did I miss anything that a colleague noticed?

* Why did I fail to notice?

Questions such as these with their responses (logged into a notebook) will assist the personal and professional development of any carer and promote valuable reflective skills.

Communication

This is not just talking or chatting to service users; indeed, it is one of the hardest skills to acquire and needs constant practice and reflection, too. Many professional carers never acquire the skills of communication to the levels desired because it is difficult, requiring constructive criticism and honest feedback from others that only a few are prepared to ask for and act upon.

The special type of listening promoted by carers is called active listening and there are many people who justifiably believe that you cannot be an effective communicator without first being an active listener. The term means that you are being active not passive in the way in which you listen; this is demonstrated by giving wholehearted attention, nodding encouragingly, prompting where necessary, clarifying any difficulties and by generally being supportive. You will find more detail about listening skills in Unit 2.

When we communicate we impart information and this may be managed more effectively if we invite questions from the audience. Sometimes speakers feel threatened by questions because they find it difficult to give answers or do not know the answer. Admit openly and honestly if you do not know the answer – do not guess or try to drive the question in a different direction without giving the answer – everyone knows what you are trying to do and will appreciate an honest reply. We have all met politicians and salespersons that have their own agendas and rarely provide direct answers to questions, particularly when they sense criticism, and they do not convince us of their credibility. Offer to search for the answer if at all possible and to return, but do not say this if you have no intention of doing so.

It is of paramount importance that you match the way you give information to the style of the service user or service user group. For example, when talking to a child or a service user with learning difficulties, it is necessary to use simple short sentences that convey the message in a positive way. For older people, especially if they have hearing difficulties, it is essential to let them see both your eyes and lips; it is usually not necessary to shout but to speak clearly and slowly. Be prepared to repeat your words, as understanding can be slower. Never use the sort of language you would use to a child; it would be quite wrong and older people may become very irritated by it.

Listen and observe how experienced carers communicate with different service users and do not be afraid to ask questions or ask for feedback.

It is also polite, especially if you are a young person, to ask the service user how he or she would like to be addressed. Just because another carer calls someone by his or her first name, you must not assume that it is all right for you to do so. Many older people may prefer to be called Mrs Smith, rather than Maggie, by someone much younger whom they have only just met. When in doubt, do not ask your friend – ask the service user.

FIGURE 1.10 *Make sure people understand your meaning*

Think it over...

Style of language must also match the service user group. Sally, who was on work experience in a residential home, was engaged in a conversation with Mrs Booth, aged 89 years; they were discussing a new cardigan, which Mrs Booth's daughter had brought on a visit the day before. Mrs Booth puzzled over Sally's comment that the cardigan was 'cool' and decided that she would never wear the garment on cold days.

Think about other fashionable language traits and how they might be misinterpreted by an older generation of service users.

Encouraging behaviour that promotes health and well-being

Encouraging service users to reinforce behaviour that increases their health and well-being (known as adaptive behaviour) is an important skill for carers. We all like praise and encouragement and will remember the occasion far longer, which increases the chances that the behaviour will be repeated and eventually become the norm. Carers should not remonstrate with service users when their behaviour is not likely to increase their well-being (known as maladaptive behaviour). The

Think it over...

Sally, who was in the last three months of pregnancy with her first child, was on the verge of being allowed to go home after being brought into antenatal care because her blood pressure was higher than it should be. Carer A met Sally re-entering the ward and stopped to speak with her. During the conversation, the carer could see the bulge of a cigarette packet in Sally's dressing gown and could smell tobacco smoke on her breath. How would you proceed with the conversation knowing that smoking increases blood pressure and seriously affects the unborn child? Practice the conversation with a colleague and ask how he or she felt.

carer can, however, gently provide information about the effects of the maladaptive behaviour, remembering that each individual is unique and free to choose.

Think it over...

Mabel Thomson, an elderly widow, had a very poor appetite following a stroke. Her medical team thought that the stroke had affected the area of her brain that controlled appetite. Consequently, already frail, she was losing weight; one day her carer noticed that she had managed to eat half of her supper and praised her by saying that she had done very well. On another occasion, an inexperienced carer gently chastised her because she had left half her meal, telling her that she would never get better if she did not eat her supper. Comment on the merits of the two carers.

Creating trust

Creating trust is vital if caring is to be a true partnership between carer and service user. A throwaway line such as 'See you later' or 'I'll be back to hear about yesterday's visit' is taken seriously by the service user, who often has little to do but wait expectantly for the carer to return. This is often seen to be of no significance by the carer beset by a hundred other issues, but the service user feels let down and of no consequence. It is far better not to not make such statements but wait and see if other duties permit, and then say 'I have a few spare minutes to hear about your visit yesterday'.

Carers and doctors, in particular, seem to have no understanding of the way in which service users or their families dissect words.

Think it over...

Mrs T telephoned the ward to see how her husband was after his heart bypass surgery. She had been told that there was no point in visiting that day, as he would be under the influence of the anaesthetic until the morning; but this did not stop her from feeling very anxious. The carer who answered the telephone paused to examine notes on a computer screen and replied that 'he was as well as could be expected'. Mrs T thanked him for the information, said she was sorry to have troubled them and put the telephone down. As she made herself a cup of tea, she thought about the reply: 'What did it mean?' 'Was Mr T not expected to recover, was he extremely ill or had some complication arisen?' Mrs T did not sleep that night because the carer's response worried her so much. How could the carer have answered Mrs T and not caused her so much anxiety?

Service users and their carers may develop special relationships when the service user reveals confidences.

Think it over...

A service user may tell a carer that she is sad that her daughter is a drug addict and had an abortion last year. She would have liked to be a grandmother. The carer tells her colleague that the daughter, who lives close to the friend, is a drug addict. Later, the colleague asks the service user if she is worried about her daughter and the service user immediately knows that her confidences have been breached. Although she does not bring up the issue with her carer, she never trusts her with information again. What are the implications for the care relationship?

In the scenario above the carer has breached confidentiality; the information had no bearing on the care of the service user and the carer had no right to pass it on to anyone without the consent of the service user. At the very least, the carer should have been disciplined and could have lost her job as a result. Every care organisation should have a policy on confidentiality, which employees must abide by.

As carers, we have the obligation to be consistent in our approach. Service users may feel angry and resentful if maladaptive behaviour is condoned one day, as it is ignored due to pressure of work, and when repeated the next day, the issue is taken up.

Think it over...

Tommy loves water play in the nursery, but he can behave badly towards other children. Yesterday, he threw a plastic cup full of water over Sarah and was forbidden to play with water again. Today, he joined the water play again and threw water over Mollie. The carer made him promise not to do it again and he continued with water play.

What effects would this inconsistency have on Sarah, Mollie and Tommy?

FIGURE 1.11 *Children in a nursery at water play*

Reducing negative feelings and behaviours of service users and others, avoiding and defusing conflict

Earlier, we looked at reflective caring and the need to notice changes in behaviour. You might notice that someone is becoming emotionally disturbed and be able to take him or her into a quiet room to enquire if they are worried about something, so managing the situation in a pro-active way. When conflict arises more suddenly, it is also wise to take the individual to a quiet place, to talk without an audience. Some people relish an audience and 'play to the gallery'. The physical act of moving also provides a few moments in which the individual may become calmer. Always keep calm yourself and try to appear confident, but do not attempt to argue or glare at the other person; dropping eye contact from time to time may also be useful. Going to fetch a supervisor, if appropriate, will give yet more time to quieten down and time to consider the issues. Use any counselling skills that you have acquired, particularly active listening skills, paraphrasing and reviewing until you are quite clear about the complaint. Use empathy and try to convey understanding of the situation; there may be a release of emotion such as crying and this release is often succeeded by a quieter period.

When appropriate, touching a hand or arm may convey a caring attitude, but be aware of any cultural differences regarding touch and any sexual implications. Never promise action that you cannot fulfil to get out of a difficult situation, and if you promise to speak to someone else (with the service user's permission) then do so promptly, again without specifying that they will take action.

Think it over...

Sam was angry. He had taken his girlfriend into A&E because she was feeling unwell, her breathing was fast and shallow and her pulse was racing. The duty medical officer asked her to breathe into a bag and several hours later sent her home having diagnosed a 'panic attack'. Two weeks later, in a different location, there was a repeat attack and this time it led to hospitalisation and a minor operation to amend the rhythm of her heart. Sam returned to the first hospital, demanding that the A&E doctor was sacked.

How would you manage Sam's anger?

Gaining compliance

This is getting someone to agree with a recommended course of action. Trying to simply persuade someone to do something usually does not work because there is no basis for agreement, only one individual trying to influence another. When that person is not present, the persuasion loses impact and the request is discarded. An individual needs information, usually in the form of reasoning or a limited number of choices in order to proceed with the request. For example, trying to persuade a service user to stop smoking will not work, but providing information on the health risks of smoking might. If this is still deemed to be too difficult, then alternatives can be offered such as reducing the number of cigarettes smoked over time with targets, providing 'patches', changing daily habits and introducing a new specific physical activity are limited choices that may be tried.

Eye contact and facial expression

These are very important in gaining compliance, because you will learn to 'read' a service user's gaze as agreeing or not. For example, an elderly male resident refuses to bathe and his table companions have complained that his body odour puts them off eating. Nobody wants to sit near him at meal times. Tom's carer decides that she will try to resolve the situation and talks to Tom in a quiet room, sitting in an open position with full eye contact to gain his attention.

Carer: 'Tom, other residents have said that your body odour prevents them enjoying their food.'

Tom: 'Who says I smell?'

Carer: 'That is not important, what is important is your personal hygiene is offending some other residents.'

Tom: 'I don't like bathing.'

Carer: 'I appreciate that, but it is necessary to wash regularly to prevent body odour caused by bacteria on the skin.'

Tom: 'I ain't got no bacteria.'

Carer: 'Everybody has bacteria on their skin, Tom, and if left too long, they produce smells, and they can cause skin infections.'

Tom: 'I don't like getting in and out of the bath, and I don't like those hoists.'

Carer: 'All right, Tom, how about a shower, where you can stand up?'

Tom: ' Well . . .'

Carer 'What about once a week?'

Tom: 'Will that stop people complaining about me?'

Carer: 'I'm sure it will, Tom, and a shower is very refreshing, you can have a special stool to sit on if you would like to.'

Tom: 'There's always someone grumbling about something.'

Carer: 'Tom, can we agree that you will take a weekly shower on, say, Tuesdays and more often if you feel like it?'

Tom: 'Oh! I suppose so.'

Tom is still a little grudging in his reply, so it is very important that eye contact is held and the last carer's statement repeated if necessary.

FIGURE 1.12 *An elderly man enjoying a sit-down shower*

Think it over...

Using the scenario above, analyse the exchange between Tom and the carer in the light of caring skills and techniques. Would you have tackled the issue differently? Justify your comments.

How might the carer follow through after the first shower day?

Eye contact and a pleasant facial expression are also important to gain someone's attention. Earlier, in the section on avoiding conflict, we discussed the importance of not glaring and even dropping eye contact when dealing with an angry person.

Disengagement

Disengagement means breaking an exchange for a short period, perhaps by going to call someone else or moving to a different location. This often has the power to calm down a heated exchange. Disengagement has been mentioned before in the section on avoiding conflict – see page 27.

Physical contact

Touching a service user's hand or arm, or putting an arm around someone's back, can be very reassuring and provides emotional security. A direct look with a smile and a touch will also show that you approve of a situation. Touching someone with whom you are unfamiliar, an individual from a different culture or a person who might consider touch to have a sexual connotation, is not to be recommended. As a carer, you will learn to resist using touch until you are sure that it will not be misinterpreted.

FIGURE 1.13 *Touching may be misinterpreted*

Distraction

This can be used to divert a service user from worrying about something too much or when they are in pain. A service user may be taught to use distraction when necessary. It may be more powerful when taught through the senses, such as concentrating on pictures or photographs and imagining sunshine or cold winds, sounds like birds singing or smells of fish and chips. This type of therapy can be combined with muscle relaxation and massage. Closing the eyes or having a blindfold can help the imagination.

The pain or the anxiety does not disappear but the mind is able to shut it out for a period, perhaps while painkillers take effect.

Modelling

This means showing only socially acceptable behaviour in a situation in the hope that a service user will learn to act in a similar way. A simple form of modelling might entail greeting service users with a warm smile and a cheery 'Good morning' on entering the room. After a few mornings, service users will greet you in the same way and often be the first to do so.

Working alongside service users

This can be a wonderful way to cement caring relationships and stimulate discussion. Playing with infants and children provides insights into the way that they relate to certain things and it has been particularly useful to use doll play in cases of suspected child abuse. People in late adulthood can be encouraged to do housework and cooking alongside caring staff to stimulate

Playing with children reveals the way they relate to others

mental activities and physical abilities. Young carers themselves can learn a lot about home-making from older people too!

Showing approval

Giving praise by making remarks such as 'Well done' or 'You look very nice today' is really valuable inside a caring relationship for it shows you noticed the effort the service user has made. Every one of us responds to praise and it is even more important with service users in care to show that they have been recognised as being human too. It is all too easy to fall into a de-humanising situation when you are doing your work. The difference here is that you are dealing with human beings with feelings.

Just because someone has a disability, illness or vulnerability does not mean that we can cease to value individuals as unique with wants, needs and hopes of their own. Just as you seek approval from parents, friends and family, service users seek approval from those nearest to them – their carers.

Setting challenges

Challenge in the form of small achievable targets is also part of the human condition. We continually set ourselves small challenges every day; for example, tomorrow I will try to get the lawn mowed, the ironing/washing done, that essay written that I have been meaning to get down to. Service users also need to be set small challenges to avoid becoming institutionalised; these may be quite simple, such as:

* walking a little bit further
* managing more personal hygiene
* playing a game
* listening to music
* doing more housework
* eating more fruit and vegetables
* spending less time in bed
* drinking more fluids.

Many other challenges may be set depending on the age, ability and experience of the service user.

Targets should always have a purpose and they are more likely to be successful when service users clearly understand the underlying reasons are for their benefit.

1.4 Services

Formal care

Many different types of services are available to potential and actual service users. Different individuals will have very differing needs and a variety of services should be available to meet those needs.

NHS services

NHS services can broadly be described as primary, secondary and tertiary. Primary services could be described as front-line services and are often the first point of contact for individuals in need. Often this is done by self-referral, that is the individual contacts the service him or herself, such as the general practitioner or the dentist. Sometimes individuals will be referred by others, such as relatives, if they are unable to do so for themselves. Secondary services are usually services to which individuals are referred by another health or social care professional. An example of this would be a lady who is suffering from arthritis in her hip. She goes to see her GP, who then refers her to an orthopaedic surgeon for further assessment and treatment. Secondary care generally focuses on hospital care, day surgeries and out-patient treatment. Tertiary care is usually specialised care such as intensive care services or long-term care such as rehabilitation or care for older people.

Community services include nursing and therapy services: district nurses, health visitors and community psychiatric nurses, for example; therapy services such as physiotherapy, occupational therapy and speech therapy and dental and optical services.

GP consultation, diagnosis and treatment

Individuals usually refer themselves to the general practitioner when they feel unwell. They will be asked to describe their symptoms and from this the GP will usually be able to make a diagnosis. It may be necessary to undertake various tests to make the diagnosis, some of which can be done at the surgery. These will include taking observations such as temperature, pulse, respiration rate and blood pressure, or taking a urine, faeces or blood sample. Generally these will need to be sent off to a laboratory for analysis, although some preliminary tests such as testing urine for glucose can be done at the surgery.

Once the GP has made a diagnosis, he or she will be able to start treatment to alleviate or cure the problem. Not all problems can be cured, but often relief can be given by different types of treatment, and the GP can refer service users to other health or social care professionals for further treatment or therapy.

Hospital services

Accident and emergency services are usually situated in large hospitals that have support services, which can be used to provide further treatment or services for individuals. People in need of emergency treatment can self-refer, or they may be referred to an accident and emergency department by a GP. Depending on the severity of the problem, individuals may be treated and discharged or may need to be admitted for further treatment. Diagnostic tools are generally more sophisticated, with more facilities available than at a GP surgery. Very ill or severely injured patients may require further diagnosis or treatment such as MRI scans or life support.

Day surgery

Day surgery is exactly what the name suggests. Individuals are admitted to a day surgery unit where they receive treatment and are discharged on the same day. This option will be considered for minor surgery; for example, some gynaecological treatments or dental extractions. Day surgery has a number of advantages, such as avoiding the need for nervous patients to spend the night in hospital, and relieving the burden on beds that might be needed for people requiring a longer stay in hospital. After-care advice must be clearly given and it must be stressed to day surgery patients that this must be followed. It is all too easy for people to believe that because their treatment has not required a stay in hospital they do not need to take time to recover. Even a small amount of general anaesthetic can make a person feel very tired for a couple of days, and many day surgery procedures will cause pain and discomfort.

Diagnosis and treatment by a hospital consultant

If a GP feels unable to provide the appropriate support and treatment for individuals, then he or she will refer them to a hospital consultant for further treatment. This is generally a senior doctor who has trained in a particular speciality for several years and is considered to be an expert in his or her field. A consultant will head a team of doctors, some of whom will still be undergoing training. Although the consultant will take overall charge of the diagnosis and treatment of patients, much of the day-to-day management of the care will be undertaken by other members of the team, and there may not be a guarantee that an operation or procedure will be carried out by the consultant in charge.

Community nursing

Community nurses provide care in the community and may provide general care or more specialised services depending on the needs of service users. District nurses are registered nurses who have an additional qualification. They may be in charge of a team of health care assistants, who provide day-to-day care in people's homes. They are usually based at GP surgeries or health centres. District nurses work closely with general practitioners and, in addition to providing care, may organise the provision of special equipment for their service users.

Community psychiatric nurses are nurses who are trained in mental-health nursing and may also have other qualifications such as a Diploma in Community Psychiatric Nursing and training in counselling and family therapy. Their role is to provide support to people who are experiencing problems in their lives or who have serious mental illnesses such as depression or schizophrenia.

Community midwives provide ante-natal and post-natal care in the community. Although most babies are born in hospital today, some mothers prefer to have their baby at home and will then require the services of the community midwife for a home delivery. Generally the midwife will take care of mother and baby for the first ten days of the baby's life, before referring them on to the health visitor.

Health Visitor

The Health Visitor is a registered nurse with special training in the assessment of the health needs of individuals, families and the community. The primary role is to promote health and tackle inequality across all age groups. Their main work is related to babies and children under five years of age. They take over the care of mother and baby when the baby is about ten days old. They run clinics, usually at GP surgeries or health centres, to monitor the children's health and undertake regular developmental checks to ensure that an individual child is developing within normal limits. The checks include hearing and sight tests. The role of the health visitor is set to change within the next few years.

Advice from NHS Direct

NHS Direct is a nurse-led 24-hour service that provides health care information and advice to the public in England on the diagnosis and treatment of common conditions through a telephone helpline and an online service. People can access the website through www.heinemann.co.uk/hotlinks (express code 1562P) to find out how to identify symptoms and by working out the course of action that is best for them. The self-help guide is also available in the back of all new Thomson Local directories.

NHS Direct Wales is a bilingual telephone help line which provides 24 hours health advice and information to people who live in Wales. The help line is manned by nurses and health information advisers who can give advice on what to do if someone is ill.

In Scotland NHS24 is a new service that became available to the whole of Scotland at the end of 2004. It is similar to NHS Direct but has the particular needs of the Scottish people in mind.

Informal care

Informal care is that given to a person in need by someone who is not paid to provide the care. Informal care is provided by a relative, neighbour or friend but can also be provided by voluntary groups such as charities or church groups.

Carers will provide all sorts of care to those they are looking after. These include:

* helping people to get up and go to bed
* helping with personal hygiene needs
* helping with toileting
* preparing food and drink
* giving medicines
* providing transport.

It is important for health care professionals to be aware that informal carers can experience high levels of stress because caring for someone, even if it is a close family member, is tiring emotionally and physically. Carers need support so that they can continue to provide the necessary care. This may include:

* having time off
* receiving satisfactory and reliable services to help them
* recognition of their role.

Early years

A variety of early years provision is available for pre-school children. This can be provided by the local authority, voluntary or private sectors. The government has pledged to provide pre-school care for all three- and four-year-olds who require it. This can take place in a variety of settings as long as it is registered by government regulatory bodies and is inspected regularly. The child registers with an early years setting, which receives funding for him or her. The minimum requirement of a part-time place is five two-and-a-half-hour sessions every week over 33 weeks (usually divided into 11-week terms). Parents have an element of choice about what type of childcare provision they have for their children. If, for example, they choose to place their child in a private fee-paying day nursery, then they will have to pay for any costs over and above the amount that is awarded for their child.

Day nurseries

These will provide full- or part-time day care for

✳ DID YOU KNOW?

In April 2001 there were 5.9 million informal carers in the United Kingdom. The majority of these carers were female (3.4 million compared with 2.5 million males). Around a quarter of both male and female carers were aged 45 to 54 with around a fifth of carers falling in each of the adjacent age groups (35 to 44 and 55 to 64).

Two-thirds of all carers were caring for less than 20 hours per week and a fifth were caring for 50 hours or more. Women were slightly more likely than men to be caring for 50 hours or more, while men were slightly more likely than women to be caring for less than 20 hours. However, of those aged 85 and over, male carers were more likely than female carers to be caring for 50 hours or more (54 per cent compared with 47 per cent).

In 2001 there were 179,000 male carers and 169,000 female carers aged 75 and over – representing 12 per cent of men within this age group and 7 per cent of women. Older men are more likely than older women to be married and therefore a larger proportion of men are able to provide care to their spouses, as well as receive care. Older women are more likely than older men to be living alone and are therefore more likely to receive care from personal social services. In Great Britain, although there was little difference between the proportions of men and women receiving home help in most age groups, a greater proportion of women than men aged 85 and over received private or local authority home help in 2001/02.

Source: Social Trends 34, 2004

children up to school age, often because parents work. They are usually private and parents pay fees. Children are given the opportunity to learn and to socialise with others.

Crèche

Crèches offer occasional care for children under the age of 8 years to give their parents the opportunity to have some time to themselves to pursue their own interests, such as going to the gym or going shopping. Parents are not usually required to stay with their child, but some may ask that the parents do not leave the building, for example in leisure centres. Crèches have to be registered if they run for more than two hours per day.

Playgroup

Playgroups are run on a not-for-profit basis and are most often managed by parent management committees. The committee employs a trained manager and trained childcare workers, but there will be parents who are involved in the day-to-day running of the service. Half the staff must be trained. Playgroups charge fees, but these are low and the average fee is approximately £3.50 for a three-hour-long session. Playgroups are registered and inspected every year.

Nursery school

A nursery school is a school for pre-school-age children, which is run independently from any other school. Nursery schools have their own head teacher and staff, which include teachers, nursery nurses and classroom assistants. A nursery school has to be registered with the government regulatory bodies and is inspected every year. It will almost certainly offer a government-approved early years curriculum. There are state nursery schools, which are free, and private nursery schools where fees are paid, although a three- or four-year-old may be entitled to a free part-time place. If a child has a free part-time place and parents wish the child to attend full-time, they would have to pay the extra cost of doing so.

Care of elderly people

In November 2003, the House of Lords Select Committee on Economic Affairs produced a report *Aspects of an Ageing Population*, and it stated that:

'The population of the United Kingdom is ageing. In 2001, for the first time in the United Kingdom, there were more people aged over 60 than under 16. By 2051, an estimated one in four people will be aged over 65. Much debate on the ageing population has focused on the challenges it presents. We believe that, just as society has adjusted to accommodate the demographic changes that have been experienced so far, so too will it adjust to accommodate the challenges of the future.'

The fact that the population is ageing will in the future provide great challenges for health and social care services, as it is probable that the needs of older people will grow. Currently, various types of provision exist that has been designed to meet the needs of older people.

Nursing and residential home care

Nursing homes are for people who have an infirmity, illness or injury that means that they require regular nursing care, which cannot be provided for them at home, and can only be provided by a registered nurse. All nursing homes must be registered and regularly inspected by the appropriate health authority, although nursing home care is usually provided by the private or voluntary sector, and not by the NHS.

Residential homes are for people who do not require nursing care but are no longer able to cope with living independently, even if they have the support of formal or informal carers.

Residential homes are provided by the local authority or private or voluntary services and all have to be registered with the appropriate social services.

Some homes are dual-registered and offer both types of care. It is important that individuals needing care are aware of the difference in the type of care offered and choose, or are helped to choose, the most appropriate care for their needs.

Day care

Day care is a valuable service offered to older people who are still able to live at home, either alone or with other members of the family, but may spend long periods of time alone during the day. It may be provided by volunteers or by the local authority. A day centre will usually provide transport to and from the centre, a range of activities and a meal. This can be a lifeline for older people who may be lonely or may have experienced abuse or neglect. Participation in the activities at a day centre, whether it is using hairdressing facilities, going on outings or even just meeting new people who become friends, will give elderly people new interests, a sense of belonging and increased self-esteem and self-confidence.

Home (domiciliary) care

There may be reasons why an individual might choose to remain living at home and receive care and support from various services. They may feel that they are still able to live at home with extra support and do not like the thought that they may lose their independence by going into residential accommodation. Many services can be provided in the community, including nursing care, help with personal hygiene or dressing, meals on wheels or a home food delivery service such as Wiltshire Farm Foods that supply ready-made frozen meals, mobile shops, library services and hairdressers. Many companies provide personal alarm systems for those who live alone. This is usually a device that is worn round the neck with a call button that when pressed, will connect with a call centre which will forward the call to a GP, relative or the ambulance service.

Needs assessment

Whenever a request is made for care for an older person, an assessment of needs should be made. This is to ensure that individual needs are identified and can be met. If an individual is thinking of going into residential care, then a needs assessment will be made to ascertain whether residential care is the only option or whether the individual would be able to stay living in his or her own home with more help and support. The assessment of needs will be made by the local social services department in the case of residential care, and by social services and a qualified health professional in the case of nursing home care.

Social services will also assess the financial status of the potential service user and this will determine whether or not the individual is entitled to some help with the cost of the fees. However, if an individual has more than £16,000 worth of assets, he or she will be expected to pay the full cost of the fees.

The needs of services users can change and needs may have to be reassessed on a regular basis. This will include a reassessment of financial status, as residential care is very expensive and a service user may find that their assets soon disappear. Once their total assets drop below £16,000 they may become entitled to help with paying the fees.

Special needs

Children and young people who have special needs such as a learning difficulty or a physical disability may have particular needs that can best be met in a special school that has the facilities and specialist staff to meet their needs. In addition to providing education, some special schools that cater for pupils with profound and multiple learning difficulties will also provide other services such as physiotherapy, speech and language therapy, sensory rooms and possibly even a hydrotherapy pool. Some special schools are for primary aged children, but some will provide education from early years to 16 or 19 years of age.

Support within mainstream schools

The Education Act 1993 stated that children with special education needs should normally be educated at mainstream schools if this is what the parents want. As a result of this, many more children with special needs are being integrated into mainstream schools. However, there are mixed feelings about this strategy which is being promoted by the government. Some people support the strategy wholeheartedly because they feel that mainstream inclusion has a positive effect on children with learning difficulties, but others feel that a child with specific educational needs may not receive the specialist support that they need, although they will often have one-to-one support from a classroom assistant. There is a fear among some parents that a child with learning difficulties may feel intimidated by the fact that they are underachieving compared with other children in the class. Children with behavioural difficulties can also cause disruption in a mainstream classroom and some would argue that this will affect the learning of all children in that class.

Summary

This section has described different types of services that are available across generations. Although each service has been described individually it is important to remember that some individuals will require care from a multidisciplinary team who work together to provide a variety of services to those in need.

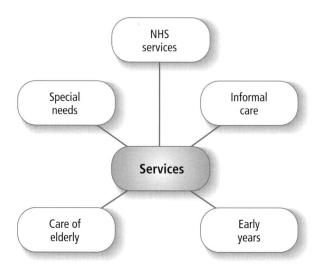

FIGURE 1.15 *Unit 1.4 summary*

> **Consider this**
>
> Undertake a survey of your local area to identify how much of the provision described above is available. Undertake research to find out what services are available and for which service user groups.
>
> Find in local newspapers any articles that relate to proposed changes to existing provision. Make sure that you identify arguments for and against the proposed changes.
>
> 1. How many different services are available?
>
> 2. What proposed changes to services did your newspaper research identify?
>
> 3. What was the reaction to the proposed changes?

1.5 Access to services

Ways in which access to services can be achieved

Different ways in which services may be accessed include:

* self-referral
* referral by a third party
* recommendation of a professional
* recall.

Self-referral

People are only able to refer themselves to services if they know that they exist. There are a variety of ways that they can find out about what is available, such as general publicity through television and newspapers, from leaflets and posters in public places and by word of mouth. Normally services for which self-referral is made are GPs, dentists, opticians or private services. People may also refer themselves to social services if they feel that they have a need, although their needs will be assessed by qualified personnel to determine whether it is sufficient to require support.

Referral by a third party

People can be referred for primary or social services by a relative, neighbour or friend. Third-party referrals can be anonymous if the person referring prefers it. Another type of third-party referral can be from one service to another, such as a district nurse referring a service user to social services.

Recommendation of a professional

Some services can only be accessed by referral from a professional. One very commonly used example of this is referral by a GP to a hospital consultant or other specialist hospital service. There are other examples of professional referral, such as the referral of a child by a teacher to an educational psychologist.

Recall

Some services will provide a recall service. This is an automatic service that comes into operation after an individual has registered with a service such as a dentist or optician, or for screening services such as breast cancer screening or cervical smear testing.

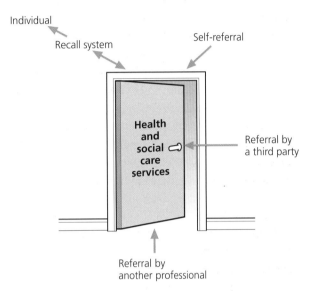

FIGURE 1.16 *Opening the door to health and social care services*

Barriers to access

There are different ways in which service users encounter barriers to receiving care from health and social care services. These are discussed below.

Inadequate resources

If there is inadequate funding and service capacity, this means that there are not enough resources to provide the care needed. This can result in delays in getting an appointment to see a general practitioner or in referral to secondary services. Staff shortages or shortage of beds can cause delays in receiving treatment and surgery, causing multiple cancellations for some individuals. Delays in receiving social service funding for residential care might result in a reduced level of care or delay in much needed care being provided. There is little that can be done about this by individual service users, but those who can afford to pay for private treatment may find that they are able to receive treatment more quickly.

Ignorance

Many people and their relatives might be completely unaware of services that may be available to them. Even if they are aware of the services, they may have no idea of how to access them. Developments in ICT, greater computer literacy and more widespread use of the Internet have helped to make information more available. In addition, public information announcements on the television are becoming more common and more people are aware of services such as NHS Direct where information can be gained by telephone or online. If people are receiving care or support from one service, careful questioning of the individual might lead the care professional to discover other needs that are not being met.

Physical difficulties

Individuals in need of services may be physically unable to access them. This may be because they live a long distance from the services they require and do not have their own transport or access to public transport. People who work full-time and have difficulty getting time off for appointments during the day may delay much needed consultations, especially if the service they require does not offer appointments before 9.00 am or after 5.00 pm.

Disabled or older people may not be able to access services due to mobility problems. If they are wheelchair users or have poor mobility, they might not be able to use public transport and may have no one they can ask to help them. Hospital car services provided by volunteers can be used to transport people to and from hospital for treatment or out-patient clinics, and social services can provide transport to take people to day centres. Various companies can provide motorised scooters for elderly people to help them to maintain their mobility, although requirements may be much simpler, such as the provision of walking sticks, frames or other mobility aids.

Communication

There are different ways in which communication can cause barriers to accessing services. If carers and service users do not have a common language it can be difficult (if not impossible) to exchange information. Service users with sensory impairments such as deafness or blindness might be prevented from accessing important information that might affect their care or physical or mental well-being. People who are illiterate will not be able to read written information and may be too embarrassed about

Reception areas should be designed to assist communication

their level of literacy to ask someone to help them. Any of these service users will suffer from inability to access services if the information they need is not available for them in suitable forms. Information could be provided in different languages and in Braille or on cassette tape. Interpreters, picture boards or signing could also be used.

Summary

In this section you have learned about the ways in which barriers can prevent full access to services that individuals require. With careful planning and knowledge of the different ways of providing information many of these barriers can be overcome. Provision of information in the right format can provide a better service to such individuals.

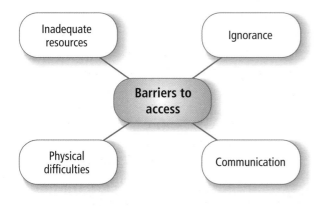

FIGURE 1.17 *Barriers to access*

Consider this

Mrs Singh is a 25-year-old Asian woman who came to live in the United Kingdom when her parents arranged her marriage four years ago. She received a basic level of education until the age of 14 but worked to help support her family until the marriage was arranged. She lives in a large city with a big Asian population and only mixes with other Asian women. As a result, she does not speak any English, only Punjabi. She has a son aged 18 months. She has just found a lump in her breast and is very worried about it. She finds it difficult to talk to her husband about such intimate matters and is reluctant to discuss it with him, partly because he works very long hours. She has confided in her next-door neighbour Mrs Kaur, who works at the local health centre. Mrs Kaur speaks Punjabi and some English and confides in the district nurse. She wants advice on how to help Mrs Singh.

1. What advice could the district nurse offer to Mrs Kaur?

2. How could the district nurse ensure that Mrs Singh receives treatment without delay?

3. What resources might the district nurse have access to that will help to provide an efficient and personalised service for Mrs Singh?

1.6 Rights and responsibilities of service users

The NHS Plan

The Prime Minister Tony Blair launched 'The NHS Plan' in July 2000 to explain how extra funding will be used to improve the NHS. 'Your Guide to the NHS' helped to explain how the changes will affect service users, what to expect now and in the future. The following information replaces The Patient's Charter, an influential document widely circulated in the 1990s. The guide (at the time of writing) may be difficult to obtain and consequently may be updated in the future.

One of the sections sets out the NHS core principles and the commitment to service users of the desire for the NHS to be a high quality health service with established aims.

The aims are listed below:

* The NHS will provide a universal service for all based on clinical need, not ability to pay

* The NHS will provide a comprehensive range of services

* The NHS will shape its services around the needs and preferences of individual patients, their families and their carers

* The NHS will respond to different needs of different populations

* The NHS will work continuously to improve quality services and to minimise errors

* The NHS will support and value its staff

* Public funds for healthcare will be devoted solely to NHS patients

* The NHS will work together with others to ensure a seamless service for patients

* The NHS will help keep people healthy and work to reduce health inequalities

* The NHS will respect the confidentiality of individual patients and provide open access to information about services, treatment and performance.

Think it over...

Consider the implications of this list of core principals for a service user and a carer in the employment of the NHS.

What does 'responding to the different needs of different populations' mean?

Discuss what you understand by 'a seamless service'.

In what ways can the NHS work to reduce health inequalities?

How can performance be judged?

Explain how confidentiality of individual patients can be respected.

Carry out a small investigation of people you know who use the services of the NHS and find out if they are aware of open access to information about services, treatment and performance.

Your commitment to the NHS

Key concept

The NHS is anxious to conserve resources and cut wastage so that all may benefit from the service. Your Guide to the NHS includes advice for service users using the service to participate in this regard. The guide also advises service users on ways to stay healthy and how to contact different sections of the NHS.

The NHS will work better if you use the service responsibly. Recommendations are made that you should:

* do what you can to look after your own health, and follow a healthy lifestyle.

* care for yourself when appropriate. (For example, you can treat yourself at home for common ailments such as coughs, colds and sore throats.)

* give blood if you are able, and carry an organ donor card or special needs card or bracelet.

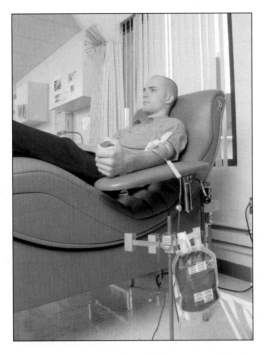

Give blood if you are able to

* listen carefully to advice on your treatment and medication. Tell the doctor about any treatments you are already taking.

* treat NHS staff, fellow patients, carers and visitors politely, and with respect. They will not accept violence, racial, sexual or verbal harassment from service users.

* keep your appointment or let the GP, dentist, clinic or hospital know as soon as possible if you cannot make it. Book routine appointments in plenty of time.

* return any equipment that is no longer needed such as crutches.

* pay NHS prescription charges and any other charges promptly when they are due and claim financial benefits or exemptions from these charges correctly.

* use this guide ('Your Guide to the NHS') to help you find the services you need.

Consider this

This is guidance for NHS service users in general. Carry out a small investigation of one or more of the bullet points, finding out whether service users know about the guidance and whether or not they abide by the principles listed. For example, you could find out whether your sample keeps appointments or treat themselves for minor ailments, donates blood or carries donor cards. Analyse your results and draw conclusions as far as you are able for a small sample. Discuss whether you think a larger sample would provide similar results.

1.7 Risks and safe working

Most occupations have some risks attached to them and workers should be trained correctly in procedures that should be taken to minimise those risks. Care workers, in particular, encounter risks because they are looking after elderly, ill or disadvantaged people and it is very important to take special protective care of their own health.

Blood-borne viruses, antibiotic-resistant bacteria, lifting injuries and violent service users are some of the major risks facing care workers.

Blood-borne viruses

HIV

The risk of contracting HIV (human immunodeficiency virus) is low providing that basic precautions are observed. Social contact has no risk attached. Sexual contact, inoculation, pregnancy/childbirth or contact with body fluids can spread the infection when there is a break in the skin or mucous membrane. Body fluids can be semen, breast milk, vaginal secretions, saliva and most importantly blood.

The most likely occurrence leading to infection of a care worker is needlestick injury. This is when a used syringe needle is accidentally plunged into a carer's own skin.

Syringe needles, scalpels and other sharp instruments used in care are collectively known as 'sharps' and special disposal methods are employed in all relevant care establishments. This is usually in a yellow 'sharps' container conforming to Department of Health standards. Other precautions are:

* strict observation of the establishment's policy on handling of equipment and material

* never replacing the needle sheath after use because this can often be the cause of needlestick injury

* leaving the needle on the syringe to minimise aerosol dispersal

* not removing scalpel blades with fingers (use forceps)

* regularly sealing sharps containers and sending for disposal (clearly labelled 'infection hazard') – daily is recommended

* wearing disposable gloves when handling sharps

* using electric shavers or depilatory cream for hair removal

* using disposable equipment whenever possible and autoclaving non-disposable items, again clearly labelled.

HIV infection continues to increase, so an increasing number of people will come into contact with carers. Many HIV positive people have no symptoms so it is wise to use gloves and plastic aprons for everyone when dealing with soiled bed linen, soiled dressings, collection of samples involving bodily fluids, intravenous drug administration, catheter care, urine bottles and bedpans. The wearing of gloves should not preclude effective hand-washing.

Normal toilet use will flush infected material away. There is no need to separate crockery from individuals with the infection unless there are open sores in the mouth or bleeding areas. Carers with cuts and abrasions should cover these with waterproof dressings and those with eczema excluded from the care of HIV+ individuals.

All body fluid splashes should be washed off immediately and if there is a perceived risk of splashing close to the face and mouth, face visors may be worn.

Soiled linen should be double-bagged (the inner bag is water-soluble and does not need to be opened) and washed at very high temperatures. The outer bag is coloured according to the organisation's guidelines.

Many HIV+ individuals suffer from feelings of discrimination and isolation so it is important to practice anti-discriminatory care and sensitivity and to remember confidentiality. HIV has a long incubation period so it is wise to use gloves and take precautions when dealing with any potential contaminated materials.

Hepatitis

There are three types of hepatitis, known as (infective) hepatitis A, (serum) hepatitis B and C; all are caused by viruses and can be serious conditions. Hepatitis A arises from poor hygiene (mouth to anus) or from infected food or drink. Hepatitis B and C are contracted through contact with infected blood or blood products and in this way have similarities with HIV infection. Immunisations are available for care workers deemed to be at risk and they should take the opportunity for added protection.

Protective measures for hepatitis are the same as those described for HIV infection.

Methicillin-resistant *Staphylococcus aureus* (MRSA)

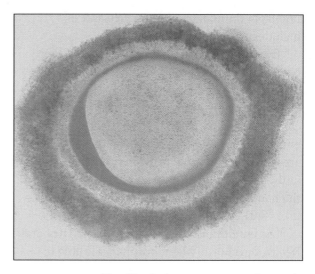

The Staphylococcus aureus bacteria

> ### Key concept
>
> *Staphylococcus aureus* are common bacteria normally colonising the skin. Strains of these bacteria have always shown an ability to be resistant to antibiotics. Methicillin, an antibiotic, was first used in the 1960s and strains of Methicillin soon started to appear; these bacteria are now called MRSA.

Some strains spread more easily than others and some people are more vulnerable than others. Media publicity surrounding service users who contract MRSA has concentrated on those who have entered hospitals for minor surgical procedures and died, or lost limbs as a result of MRSA infections.

Politicians, both past and present, are blamed for dirty hospitals associated with MRSA and poor contract cleaning to reduce costs. The Secretary of State for Health has declared that

MRSA infection levels are beginning to decline as new measures take effect (March 2005).

MRSA is resistant to all penicillin drugs and can be resistant to other antibiotics as well; this means that only a small range of other antibiotics is available to treat service users who have these infections. These can be difficult to give, expensive and toxic to the service user. MRSA complications are unpredictable, so taking a standardised approach appropriate for all service users is not possible.

Some people carry MRSA on and in their bodies without harmful effects, but those who are more vulnerable can have life-threatening complications. Vulnerable people who are most at risk include:

* people in intensive care units

* surgical patients who have undergone invasive procedures

* service users who have had recent antibiotic treatment

* service users who have just been in hospital.

It is not known how many people in the community carry MRSA; certainly many people visiting those in hospital will be carriers of MRSA and some care workers themselves will be MRSA+. There is also potential infection in residential and nursing homes and their care staff. It makes sense that basic principles of care must underpin foundations for practice and this includes preventing cross-infection.

The most important principles behind the control of cross-infection are effective hand washing and good hygiene.

Good-quality soap, running clean water and careful drying are often all that is necessary for effective hand hygiene. However, most at-risk areas in hospitals now provide a suitable antiseptic/detergent soap and alcohol gel rub for the hands. This is available for care staff, service users and visitors to use at appropriate times.

The environment must be kept clean, dry and free from rubbish. Many hospitals are able to provide guidance leaflets for staff, service users and visitors.

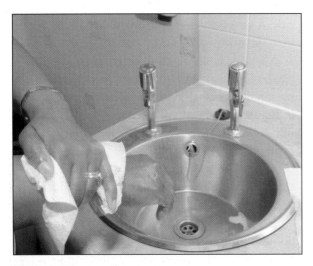

FIGURE 1.19 *Effective hand-washing prevents cross-infection*

Think it over...

Discuss the appropriate times for effective hand washing, bearing in mind the normal location of MRSA bacteria and the likely contaminated material from MRSA+ service users. You will find more useful information on page 10.

Matrons have been appointed to oversee cleanliness in care establishments, particularly where contract cleaners are still in place. Other establishments have taken back their own cleaning in order to have more control. In November 2004, Dr John Reid Secretary of State for Health gave an undertaking to halve the rates of MRSA infection by 2008 and charged Primary Health Care Trusts with the responsibility.

Think it over...

Talk to people you know, service users or those who visit relatives or friends in care establishments and ask them about cleanliness and tidiness in the wards. Collect media articles on MRSA and dirty hospitals and find out through government statistics whether MRSA is in decline.

Lifting injuries

Lifting injuries have been one of the main problems of care workers for decades. You should never try to move or lift a service user without correct training by an authorised tutor of moving and handling techniques. You must decline politely if you are not trained since you would place both your service user and yourself at risk of permanent damage. This is particularly so if you are an adolescent or young adult as your skeleton is still forming.

Think it over...

You should be aware of the following acts, regulations and polices:

* Health and Safety at Work Act (1974)
* Manual Handling Operations Regulations (1992)
* RCN guidelines for moving and handling
* European guidelines on moving and handling (various)
* Management of HASAW (1992)
* Lifting Operations and Lifting Equipment Regulations (1998)
* Local policies in the care establishment that you visit or do a work placement in.

Studying manual handling from a guide or textbook is not a substitute for the training course.

Imagine you are trying to learn how to ride a bicycle. No amount of reading can enable you to get on a cycle and ride perfectly straight away. The volume of legislation identifies the degree of concern that governments, trade unions, employers and employees have over lifting injuries. Although the problem exists in many professions, care workers have experienced a greater incidence of injury than any other.

People do not come in neat tidy packages, service users have fears and anxieties about being moved and many service users were not encouraged to help themselves, as is the case now. In the past, lifting aids were not numerous; most care workers were young women with unsuitable uniforms for lifting. Everything is relatively different today. Manual handling is kept to a minimum with whole-body or near whole-body lifts being eliminated for safety. Lifting aids are plentiful and carers are trained in their use. When manual lifts are unavoidable, trained carers work in teams and nurses, in particular, are encouraged to wear trousers so that more suitable stances can be taken for weight-bearing. Beds are now more moveable and the height is easy to adjust.

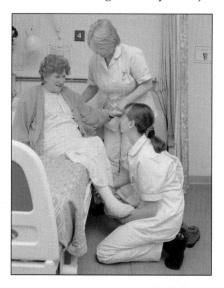

Nurses wearing trousers

Certain people in each hospital location or sub-location are designated to oversee the manual handling and most carers, after being trained, are required to undergo regular refresher courses to ensure that no bad habits have crept into their procedures.

Before an unavoidable lift, the risks are assessed and a plan is formulated; this includes the use of mechanical aids and the number of helpers. The team and the service user must be fully informed about each step of the lift. When the service user is able to give assistance, this is incorporated into the plan. A fully informed service user is more relaxed and cooperative and knows what to expect.

> ## ✳ DID YOU KNOW?
>
> Many lift types used in the past, such as the Drag lift and the Australian lift have now been condemned by the Royal College of Nursing, so keeping up to date with the latest thinking has never been more important.
>
> Most injuries caused by lifting affect the lower back and previously most nurses had been affected by low back pain at some time in their careers.

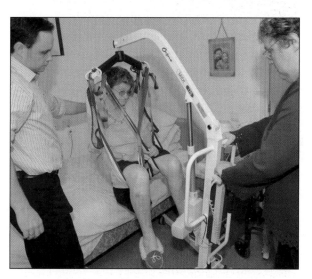

A service user being lifted using mechanical aids

Violence from service users

We all live in what appears to be a more violent and aggressive society and this is clearly shown in the increasing number of violent and aggressive incidents that care workers have to deal with on a daily basis. Nurses appear to be more than five times at risk of abusive behaviour than those who work in other occupations. The majority of unacceptable behaviour stems from service users in accident and emergency units and psychiatric wards. Community nurses are also vulnerable as they work in service users' homes but no care department seems to be exempt. Verbal abuse is the most common but minor and severe injuries occur as well.

Many care establishments, particularly hospitals open 24 hours, have invested in closed-circuit television and this has proved to be a deterrent. Service users who are intoxicated with alcohol also form one of the main problems in A&E units.

Some primary health care trusts refuse to treat service users who abuse staff (see also 'Your commitment to the NHS' on page 40) for a set period of time, often one year. Letters are sent to the service user's GP to confirm this.

As a learner, you should not be working on your own with a service user in a restricted space, but you should still know the basic precautions for your own safety.

Inappropriate behaviour is behaviour not usually seen in the care setting; often distressing, sometimes violent, occasionally oppressive or simply ignoring the needs of others around are examples of such behaviour. Inappropriate behaviour can come from service users, visitors or care workers. In some cases you will be able to understand why the individual is acting in this manner, in other cases you will not. Understanding the reasons or circumstances behind the behaviour does not change its unacceptability. In most cases you will be able to refer the matter to a supervisor, as you should not be working on your own. There are certain generic guidelines for dealing with inappropriate behaviour, but you must realise that each situation will be unique and sizing up the problem quickly will help.

Try to anticipate trouble and defuse it before it happens; knowing your service users will help you to do this.

Think it over...

Mr J, an ex-army man with a brusque manner, is a service user in the residential home in which you are working for two weeks' vocational placement. He likes to sit in a particular chair to watch the television in the communal living room. A new service user, Mrs M, came into the room straight after the evening meal, and occupied Mr J's chair. Mrs M is a timid service user, who has become prone to bouts of weeping since her husband died. You anticipate the problem that might arise when Mr J enters. How will you approach Mrs M and what might you say to her? Is it necessary to refer the matter to a supervisor?

Although Mr J is brusque and may distress Mrs M a great deal he is not likely to be violent. Most of the generic guidelines above will be appropriate for dealing with violent people as well, but in addition you will need to know:

* how to get out of the space as quickly as possible
* how to summon help – sound an alarm, shout for help, call security or police
* not to let an attacker get between you and the door
* remove any potential weapons if it is easy to do so.

Above all, keep yourself safe; you are a student and not trained to deal with attackers. Even if there are other people such as service users in the room, as an untrained person you will be more use bringing trained staff to their aid.

Think it over...

Find out about the appropriate steps to take in your placement when dealing with aggression and violence by reading the policy document and observing how other people manage sensitive situations.

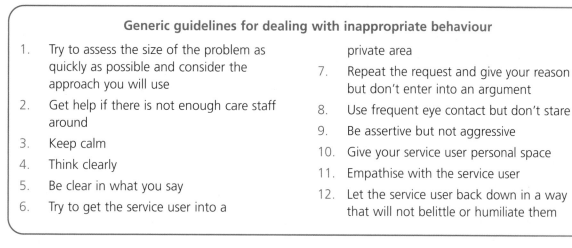

Generic guidelines for dealing with inappropriate behaviour

1. Try to assess the size of the problem as quickly as possible and consider the approach you will use
2. Get help if there is not enough care staff around
3. Keep calm
4. Think clearly
5. Be clear in what you say
6. Try to get the service user into a private area
7. Repeat the request and give your reason but don't enter into an argument
8. Use frequent eye contact but don't stare
9. Be assertive but not aggressive
10. Give your service user personal space
11. Empathise with the service user
12. Let the service user back down in a way that will not belittle or humiliate them

Abuse

Sitting alongside inappropriate behaviour, there is the problem of abuse. This can be in many forms as shown in Figure 1.20.

- Physical abuse
- Sexual abuse
- Abuse by neglect
- **Forms of abuse**
- Psychological abuse
- Emotional abuse
- Financial abuse or exploitation

FIGURE 1.20 *Some forms of abuse*

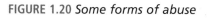

Consider this

Over a period of three months collect cuttings/photocopies from newspapers or magazines, or refer to TV documentaries related to different forms of abuse. Obtain a copy of one placement's policy on dealing with abuse.

In a small group discuss a selection of cases in the following ways:

✳ Which service user group was being abused?

✳ How many service users were involved?

✳ Who were the abusers?

✳ What type of care setting was involved?

✳ How long did the abuse continue?

✳ What were the likely short- and long-term effects on the service user?

✳ What signs might you have noticed if you had been working in that care setting?

✳ Why do you think the abuse started?

✳ What could you have done about it? (Your placement policy can be used here.)

You might find it helpful to repeat this exercise again using different cases before your study programme is finished to reinforce the importance of awareness of abuse.

You will be assessed on your knowledge, understanding and skills relating to effective caring through a written examination of one and a half hours.

Test questions

1. What factors must care workers take into account if they wish to ensure that their way of communicating is effective? (4)

2. Describe how distraction can be used to help a service user combat chronic pain. (3)

3. Explain the value of setting challenges for an older adult recovering from a hip replacement. (4)

4. A newly employed care worker takes a phone call from a man claiming to be Mr Sanderson, the son of a resident. He says that he has heard that his mother is very ill and wants to know what is wrong with her. What factors should the care worker take into account and what action should he or she take? (3)

5. Mrs B has had her operation cancelled twice; this time she had been prepared for theatre in the morning before being told that it had been cancelled again. Mr B has arrived to visit his wife and found that he is to take her home again without surgery. He is furious and threatens to punch the nearest person on duty, which is you. Explain how you would manage the situation. (5)

6. Ten year old George has just arrived home from school very excited because he has won a national prize in a story writing competition. His mother is watching day-time television and tells him not to disturb her. When he tries to get her to listen, she shouts that she has already told him not to disturb her and sends him to his bedroom. Explain how she is not treating George well. (5)

7. Identify and explain the precautions you would take helping a nurse colleague to change the soiled linen from a bed of a service user who has recently had surgery and is known to have hepatitis B. (5)

8. Define primary, secondary and tertiary care. (3)

9. Identify the physical difficulties service users may experience accessing health or social care services. (4)

10. Describe the precautions designed to minimise lifting injuries in care staff. (5)

References

Department of Health (2000) *Your Guide to the NHS*, NHS London

R. Rogers, J. Salvage (1998) *Nurses at Risk*, Palgrave Macmillan, Basingstoke

The Terrence Higgins Trust for information on HIV and Aids

NUPE, trade union for information on health and safety of health care workers

R. Adams (1994) *Skilled work with people*, Collins Educational, London

B. Hopson, M. Scally (1994) *Communication, Time to Talk*, Mercury, London

A. Pease, B. Pease, (2005) *The Definitive Book of Body Language*, Sheldon Press, London

P. Burnard (1992) *Communicate!* Hodder Arnold, London

A. Jaskolka (2004) *How to Read and Use Body Language*, Foulsham, London

N. Moonie (2000), *AVCE Health and Social Care*, Heinemann, Oxford

Y. Nolan (2001), *S/NVQ Care Level 3*, Heinemann, Oxford

Useful websites

Please see www.heinemann.co.uk/hotlinks (express code 1562P) for links to the following websites which may provide a source of information:

* Health Development Agency

* NHS Direct Wales

* NHS Direct

* NHS 24

Effective communication

You will learn about:

2.1 Types of communication

2.2 Communication difficulties and strategies to overcome these

2.3 Barriers to communication and factors affecting the effectiveness of communication skills

2.4 Communication when working in teams

2.5 Clients and care settings

2.6 Giving a talk

2.7 Feedback research

2.8 Evaluating communication skills

Introduction

This unit focuses on communication skills. It explores different types of communication, together with some of the factors that affect the effectiveness of communication skills. Communication skills relevant to specific service user groups and care settings are discussed in depth. For this unit you are required to produce a report based on a short talk that you will prepare and give to a small audience. This talk should be about good practice in communication skills for one type of service user in one care setting.

How you will be assessed

This unit is internally assessed. You will need to produce a report based on a short talk which you will prepare and present to a small audience.

2.1 Types of communication

We use words when we speak – oral communication; and we use words when we write – written communication.

Oral or verbal communication

Thompson (1986) writing about health work, argues that communication is important for two major reasons. Firstly, communication enables people to share information, and secondly, communication enables relationships between people. Teresa Thompson states that 'communication is the relationship' (1986: 8). Speaking or signing is central to establishing relationships between people and care workers need to have highly developed social skills in order to work with the wide range of emotional needs that service users will have. Face-to-face, oral (or mouth) communication involves using words and sentences (verbal communication) together with a range of body language messages (non-verbal communication).

Oral communication may be central to the kind of tasks listed in Figure 2.1.

Oral communication is central to emotional work as well as communicating information

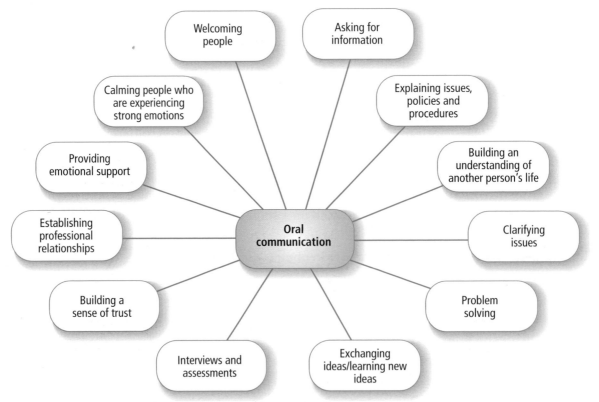

FIGURE 2.1 *Examples of tasks for which oral communication is central*

Written communication

There is an old Chinese saying that the weakest ink is stronger than the strongest memory! Written records are essential for communicating formal information that needs to be reviewed at a future date. When people recall conversations they have had, they will probably miss some details out, and also change some details. Written statements are much more permanent and if they are accurate when they are written they may be useful at a later date.

Some examples of important written documents are listed in Figure 2.2.

When an issue is recorded in writing it becomes formal. It is important that records of personal information are as factual and accurate as possible. You should describe only the facts or the events that happened, without giving your own interpretation or saying how you feel about the person.

Many organisations use printed forms to help staff to ask important questions and check that they have taken accurate information. Service users' personal records are likely to be written on forms that use headings.

Non-verbal communication – Para language

Tone of voice

Tone involves the way our voice resonates as we speak. It is not just what we say, but the way that we say it. If we talk quickly in a loud voice with a fixed voice tone, people may see us as angry. In most UK contexts, a calm, slow voice with varying tone may send a message of being friendly. A sharp tone may be associated with angry or complaining behaviour. A flat tone might be associated with exhaustion or depression. A faint tone might be associated with submissive behaviour.

Pitch

Pitch relates to the sound frequency of the voice. Some people might speak in a monotonous high-frequency voice or a monotonous low-frequency voice. It is important to vary the type of sound

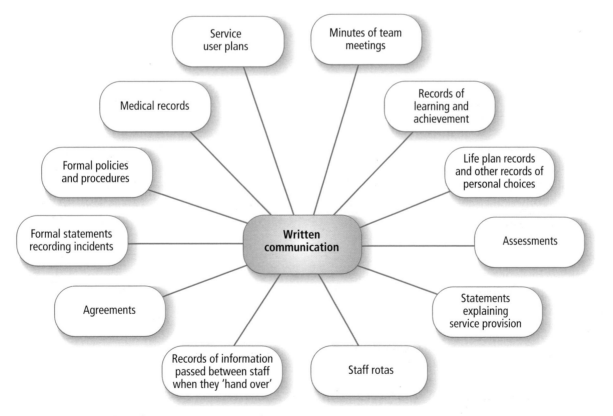

FIGURE 2.2 *Examples of important written documents*

that we make. And culturally there may be expectations as to how high or low our voice should sound.

Speed of speech

Bostrom (1997) states that announcers (such as radio or TV presenters) speak at a rate of between 100 and 125 words per minute. This speed might represent an ideal pace for explaining information. A great deal of speech is used to express emotional reaction rather than simply explaining issues to an audience. A faster speed of speech might indicate that the speaker is excited, anxious, agitated, nervous, angry or seeking to impress or dominate the listener. Alternatively, a fast speed might simply mean that the speaker is in a hurry!

Exactly what a fast rate of speaking means can only be worked out by interpreting other non-verbal body language and the cultural context and situation of the speaker. People who wave their arms, wide eyed and smiling, while talking rapidly about exam results might be interpreted as being excited at the news of having done well.

A slow speed of speech can indicate sadness or depression. Slow speech may sometimes be associated with impairment of thought processes. Slow speech might indicate tiredness or boredom. Slow, loudly spoken speech might be used to convey dominance or hostility. Sometimes slow speech can indicate attraction, love and affection between individuals who know each other. Once again, this aspect of communication can only be interpreted once the non-verbal, social, cultural and practical context of the conversation is understood.

In formal communication work, such as, for example, if you were meeting people at an information desk or hospital reception, it might be important to maintain a normal pace of speech. This is because your work might focus on a formal exchange of information. Informal situations often involve a need to communicate emotions, such as, for example, talking to a service user you know well. In this situation you might want to speak faster or slower in order to communicate your emotions clearly.

Volume – how loud you speak

Talking or shouting loudly often sends a message that you are excited, angry or aggressive, unless you are in a situation where it is obvious that you are trying to overcome background noise or communicate with someone who is a long distance away. Talking quietly sometimes sends a message that you lack confidence, or that you are being submissive in the presence of a more important person. Once again, talking quietly is an obvious strategy if you do not want everybody to hear what you are saying.

Clarity of voice

It is important not to mumble, slur or drawl our words when speaking, and also not to stress words inappropriately, or clip words when speaking if we are to communicate effectively. Clarity of voice can be affected by our emotional state and many people need to imagine themselves speaking clearly in order to achieve a clear voice.

Hesitation

In order to speak clearly we need to think through what we are about to say. A long pause in which nothing is said is often interpreted as an indication that the speaker has finished talking. One way of showing that you intend to continue speaking is to use sounds such as 'uhm' and 'ah' so that it is obvious that you intend to continue speaking, even though you are not actually communicating. In an informal setting, friendly listeners can often cope with this behaviour. When giving a formal speech, too many 'uhms' or other meaningless pause fillers may mean that listeners lose track of the content of your communication.

Non-verbal communication – body language

When meeting and talking with people we usually use two language systems. These are:

* a verbal or spoken language

* a non-verbal or body language.

Effective communication in care work requires that care workers have the ability to analyse their own and other people's non-verbal behaviour. Our body sends messages to other people – often without our deliberately meaning to send these messages. Some of the most important body areas that send messages are outlined below.

Body language (see Figure 2.3). The way we use our body can communicate messages to other people. People communicate with one another using words and also by using body language.

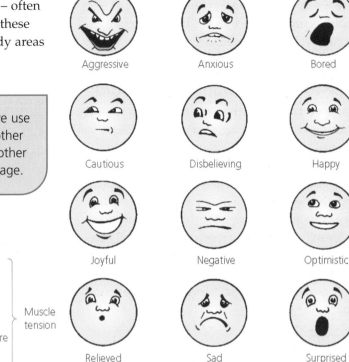

FIGURE 2.4 *Facial expression*

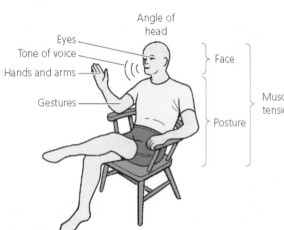

FIGURE 2.3 *The use of body language*

Eye contact

We can guess the feelings and thoughts that another person has by looking at their eyes. One poet called the eyes 'the window of the soul'. We can sometimes understand the thoughts and feelings of another person by eye-to-eye contact. Our eyes get wider when we are excited, attracted to, or interested in someone else. A fixed stare may send the message that someone is angry. Looking away is often interpreted as being bored or not interested, in European culture.

Facial expression

Our face can send very complex messages and we can read them easily – see Figure 2.4.

Our face often indicates our emotional state. When people are sad they may signal this emotion with eyes that look down; there may be

tension in their face, and their mouth will be closed. The muscles in the person's shoulders are likely to be relaxed but the face and neck may show tension. A happy person will have 'wide eyes' that make contact with you and a smiling face. When people are excited they may move their arms and hands to signal this emotion.

Proximity and personal space

The space between people can sometimes show how friendly or 'intimate' the conversation is. Different cultures have different assumptions about how close people should be (proximity) when they are talking.

In Britain there are expectations or 'norms' as to how close you should be when you talk to others. When talking to strangers we may keep an arm's-length apart. The ritual of shaking hands indicates that you have been introduced and you may move closer. When you are friendly with someone you may accept their being closer to you. Relatives and partners may not be restricted in how close they can come.

Personal space is a very important issue in care work. A care worker who assumes it is all right to enter a service user's personal space without asking or explaining, may be seen as being dominating or aggressive.

Face-to-face positions (orientation)

Standing or sitting eye to eye can send a message of being formal or being angry. A slight angle can create a more informal, relaxed and friendly feeling (see Figure 2.5).

If you are facing an audience of people in order to deliver a formal talk you might wish to face your audience 'squarely' or eye to eye in order to look confident, prepared and ready to deliver your talk. The further your audience are away from you, the less they will be able to see your face and eye contact and the less feedback

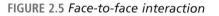

FIGURE 2.5 *Face-to-face interaction*

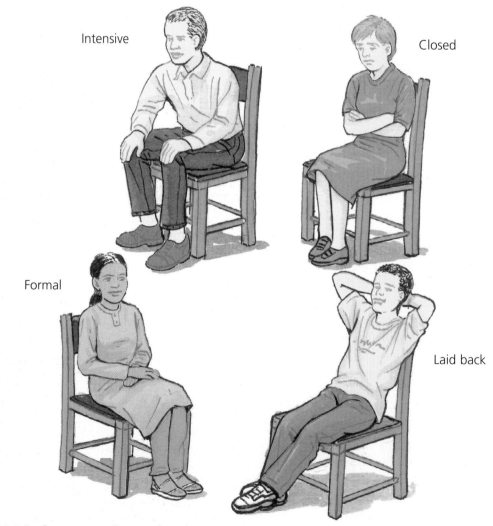

Intensive

Closed

Formal

Laid back

FIGURE 2.6 *Body postures that send messages*

you will get from them. This creates more formality. Again, if you are some distance from your audience you will need to increase the volume of your voice in order to be heard clearly. As a general rule – a rule that is not always right – the larger the group you are talking to, and the further away you are, the more formal your body language will need to become.

Body movement

The way we walk, move our head, sit, cross our legs and so on, sends messages about whether we are feeling tired, happy, sad or bored.

Posture

The way we sit or stand can send messages. Sitting with crossed arms can mean 'I'm not taking any notice'. Leaning back can send the message that you are relaxed or bored. Leaning forward can show interest. The body postures shown in Figure 2.6 send messages.

Muscle tension

The tension in our feet, hands and fingers can tell others how relaxed or how tense we are. When people are very tense their shoulders might stiffen, their face muscles might tighten and they might sit or stand rigidly. A tense face might have a firmly closed mouth with lips and jaws clenched tight. A tense person might breathe quickly and become hot.

Gestures

Gestures are hand and arm movements that can help us to understand what a person is saying. Some gestures carry a meaning of their own. Some common gestures are shown below.

'I don't know'

'stop, don't do that'

'success – everything's going well'

'perfection' or 'perfect'

FIGURE 2.7 *Some gestures common in Britain*

2.2 Communication difficulties and strategies to overcome these

Sensory impairments of vision and hearing

Some service users will have sensory impairments such as impaired vision or hearing. Many people who are 'registered blind' can sense some images and can tell the difference between light and darkness. However, low vision often means that a person cannot see your non-verbal behaviour. Because of this, it is important to remember that a person with low vision may not understand your emotions unless you can communicate using your tone of voice. It will also be important to remember to explain things that sighted people take for granted. For example, an explanation of issues like the weather may benefit people with low vision, though obvious to a sighted person.

Many older service users lose the ability to hear high-pitched sounds, although they can still hear low-frequency sound. This means that many older people have difficulty in understanding some speech. Sometimes a service user may understand their relatives because they are used to their style of speaking and may even be able to read their lips. A service user may have difficulty understanding the speech, or the lip movements of somebody whom they do not know. People who have been Deaf since birth often learn to use British Sign Language and they therefore have a different language to English. Learning to sign is a useful skill for communicating with members of the Deaf community. People who develop a hearing impairment in later life are unlikely to have learned British Sign Language. Many people with a hearing loss may prefer to communicate using speech and reading replies written in English if they cannot interpret non-verbal communication and the sounds that others make.

Aphasia

Aphasia is a disability that can involve an inability to speak and/or an inability to understand spoken language. Certain types of head injury can result in aphasia. A person with expressive aphasia may be able to understand language but unable to respond with speech. A person with receptive aphasia may be unable to understand what you are saying. Sometimes a person who cannot speak can nevertheless answer your questions using signs, pointing to pictures or even writing answers.

Overcoming communication difficulties

British Sign Language

The British Deaf Association states that British Sign Language 'is the first or preferred language of nearly 70,000 Deaf people in the United Kingdom'. The British Deaf Association explains that British Sign Language (BSL) 'belongs to Deaf people. It is not a communication system devised by hearing people. It is a real language which has evolved in the UK's Deaf community over hundreds of years'. The British Deaf Association campaign for the right of Deaf people to be educated in BSL and to access information and services through BSL, arguing that the Deaf community is a 'linguistic and cultural minority and is not measured in medical terms'.

Note: the use of a capital 'D' in Deaf is deliberate. It denotes culturally Deaf. Culturally Deaf means that deafness is about belonging to a different language community – and not about being an impaired-hearing person.

Please see www.heinemann.co.uk/hotlinks (express code 1562P) for further details about BSL, signs and finger spelling alphabet, and the website of the Royal Association for Deaf People.

Makaton

Makaton is a system for developing language that uses speech, signs and symbols to help people with learning difficulties to communicate and to develop their language skills. People who communicate using Makaton may speak a word and perform a sign using hands and body language. There is a large range of symbols that may help people with learning difficulty to recognise an idea or to communicate with others. Further information on Makaton can be found at www.heinemann.co.uk/hotlinks (express code 1562P).

Braille

Braille (a system of raised marks that can be felt with your fingers) provides a system of written communication based on the sense of touch for people who have limited vision. The communication system known as Braille was first published by Louis Braille, a blind 20-year-old, in 1829. The system is now widely adopted as the form of writing and reading used by people who cannot see written script.

Nowadays, computer software can translate written material into Braille, which can be printed out using special printers. Further detail on Braille can be found at www.heinemann.co.uk/hotlinks (express code 1562P).

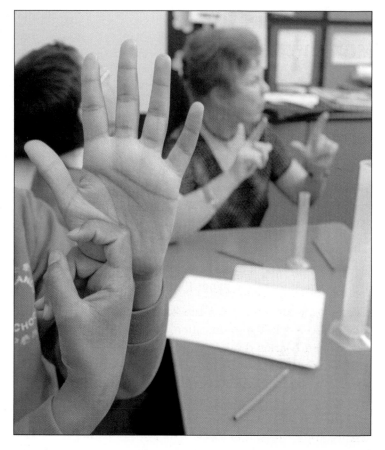

Sign language is used by nearly 70,000 Deaf people in the UK

2.3 Barriers to communication and factors affecting the effectiveness of communication skills

Communication can become blocked if individual differences are not understood. The three main ways that communication becomes blocked are:

1. A person cannot see, hear or receive the message.
2. A person cannot make sense of the message.
3. A person misunderstands the message.

Examples of the first kind of block, where people do not receive the communication, include visual disabilities, hearing disabilities, environmental problems such as poor lighting, noisy environments, and when speaking from too far away.

> ## Key concept
>
> *Barriers:* effective communication depends on identifying barriers that may block understanding. Barriers can exist at a physical and sensory level, at the level of making sense of a message and at a cultural and social context level where the meaning of a message may be misunderstood.

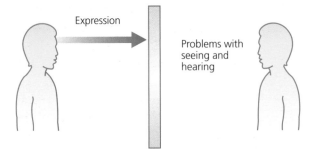

Expression

Problems with seeing and hearing

FIGURE 2.8 *Environmental problems like noise and poor light can create communication barriers*

Examples of situations in which people may not be able to make sense of the message include:

* the use of different languages, including signed languages
* the use of different terms in language, such as jargon (technical language), slang (different people using different terms), or dialect (people from different communities use different sounds to say words)
* physical and intellectual disabilities, such as dysphasia (difficulties with language expression or understanding, aphasia (an absence of language ability) being ill, or suffering memory loss, or learning difficulty.

Reasons for misunderstanding a message include:

* cultural influences – different cultures interpret non-verbal and verbal messages, and humour, in different ways
* assumptions about people – about race, gender, disability and other groupings
* labelling or stereotyping of others
* social context – statements and behaviour that are understood by friends and family may not be understood by strangers
* emotional barriers – a worker's own emotional needs may stop them from wanting to know about others
* time pressures can mean that staff withdraw from wanting to know about others
* emotional differences can sometimes be interpreted as personality clashes, or personality differences. Very angry, or very happy, or very shy people may misinterpret communication from others.

In order to minimise communication barriers it will be important to learn as much as possible about others. People may have 'preferred forms of interaction'. This may include a reliance on non-verbal messages, sign language, lip-reading, the use of description, slang phrases, choice of room or location for a conversation and so on. Everyone has communication needs of some kind.

Different language systems

When people use different language systems there may be an obvious barrier to understanding. It may be necessary to use the services of an interpreter or translator in order for people to communicate across a language barrier. Interpreters are people who communicate meaning from one language to another. Translators are people who change recorded material from one language to another.

Translating and interpreting involve the communication of meaning between different languages. Translating and interpreting are not just the technical acts of changing the words from one system to another. Many languages do not have simple equivalence between words or signs. Interpreters and translators have to grasp the meaning of a message and find a way of expressing this meaning in a different language system. This is rarely a simple task even for professional translators.

Interpreters can be professional people but they may also be friends, or family members. For example, a mother might learn sign language in order to communicate information to a Deaf child. It is sometimes possible for family members to interpret for each other.

Terminology

The actual words or terms that you use will influence both what another person understands and the relationship that you have with the person you are communicating with. Words can create a sense of formality or informality. The use of technical terminology also identifies the social groups that you identify with.

The degree of formality or informality is called the language 'register'. For example, suppose you went to a hospital reception. You might expect the person on duty to greet you with a formal response such as, 'Good morning, how can I help you?'. An informal greeting of the kind used by white males in the south-east of England might be, 'Hello, mate, what's up then?' or 'How's it going?'. It is possible that some people might prefer the informal greeting. An informal greeting could put you at ease; you might feel that the receptionist is like you. But in many situations, the informal greeting might make people feel that they are not being respected.

The degree of formality or informality establishes a context. At a hospital reception you are unlikely to want to spend time making friends and chatting things over with the receptionist. You may be seeking urgent help. Your expectations of the situation might be that you want to be taken seriously and put in touch with professional services as soon as possible. You might see the situation as a very formal encounter.

If you are treated informally, you may interpret this as not being treated seriously, or in other words 'not being respected' (see Figure 2.9).

FIGURE 2.9 *Informality and informal humour may be perceived as disrespect*

Speech communities

Another issue is that informal speech is very likely to identify a specific speech community. Different localities, ethnic groups, professions and work cultures all have their own special words, phrases and speech patterns. An elderly, middle-class woman is very unlikely to start a conversation with the words 'Hello, mate'. Some service users may feel threatened or excluded by the kind of language they encounter. However, the use of formal language in itself will not solve this problem. The technical terminology used by social care workers may also create barriers for people who were not part of that 'speech community'.

Think it over...

Service user:	I come about getting some help around the house, you know, 'cause it's getting 'ard nowadays, what with me back an everything.
Service worker:	Well you need to speak to the Community Domiciliary Support Liaison Officer, who can arrange an assessment in accordance with our statutory obligations.

The two statements above use different levels of formality, but they also represent speech from different speech communities. Can you work out what each person is saying? How do you think the service user will feel given such a response? Will the service user feel respected and valued?

Cultural beliefs and assumptions

Skilled carers have to get to know the people that they work with in order to avoid making false assumptions about them. In getting to know an individual, carers will also need to understand the ways in which class, race, age, gender and other social categories influence the person. A person's culture may include all social groups that they belong to.

There are many different ethnic groups in the world, many different religions, many different cultural values, variations in gender role, and so on. Individuals may belong to the same ethnic group, yet belong to different religions or class groups. Knowing someone's religion will not necessarily tell you all of their beliefs, or about their general culture.

You can acquire background knowledge on different ethnic and religious customs, but it is impossible to study and learn about all the differences that can exist for individual service users. The best way to learn about diversity is to listen and communicate with people who lead very different lives.

It is important to be able to identify the different interpretations that words and body language have in different cultures. This is not a straightforward issue, as words and signs can mean different things depending on their context. For example, the word 'wicked' can have different meanings. If older people use this phrase to describe their experience of World War II, it would mean 'horrific' or 'terrible'. In a TV comedy written and produced 15 years ago the

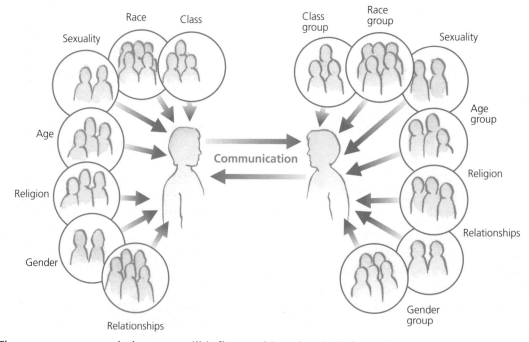

FIGURE 2.10 *The groups a person belongs to will influence his or her beliefs and behaviour*

phrase would mean 'cool' – something very desirable. In a religious context 'wicked' might relate to the concept of sin.

Making sense of spoken language requires knowledge of the context and intentions of the speaker. Understanding non-verbal communication involves exactly the same need to understand 'where the person is coming from' or, to put it more formally, to understand what the circumstances and cultural context of the other person are. For example, in Britain the hand gesture with palm up and facing forward means 'Stop, don't do that'. In Greece it can mean 'You are dirt' and is a very rude gesture.

Why do the same physical movements have different meanings? One explanation for the hand signs is that the British version of the palm-and-fingers gesture means 'I arrest you, you must not do it'; whereas the Greek interpretation goes back to medieval times when criminals had dirt rubbed in their faces to show how much people despised them.

Using care values means that carers must have respect for other people's culture. People learn different ways of communicating, and good carers will try to understand the different ways in which people use non-verbal messages. For instance, past research in the USA suggests that white and black Americans may have used different non-verbal signals when they listened. It suggests that some black Americans may tend not to look much at the speaker. This can be interpreted as a mark of respect – by looking away it demonstrates that you are really thinking hard about the message. Unfortunately, not all white people understood this cultural difference in non-verbal communication. Some individuals misunderstood and assumed that this non-verbal behaviour meant exactly what it would mean if they had done it. That is, it would mean they were not listening.

Key concept

Cultural assumptions: communication is always influenced by cultural systems of meaning. Different cultures interpret body language differently.

There is an almost infinite variety of meanings that can be given to any type of eye contact, facial expression, posture or gesture. Every culture develops its own special system of meanings. Carers have to understand and show respect and value for all these different systems of sending messages. But how can you ever learn them all?

No one can learn every possible system of non-verbal message – but it is possible to learn about those that people you are with are using! It is possible to do this by first noticing and remembering what others do – i.e. what non-verbal messages they are sending. The next step is to make an intelligent guess about what messages the person is trying to give you. Finally, check your understanding (your guesses) with the person.

Skilled interpersonal interaction involves:

∗ watching other people,

∗ remembering what they do

∗ guessing what words and actions mean and then checking your guesses with the person

∗ never relying on your own guesses, because these might turn into assumptions

∗ understanding that assumptions can lead to discrimination.

Think it over...

Imagine you are working with an older person. Whenever you start to speak to her she always looks at the floor and never makes eye contact. Why is this?

Your first thought is that she might be depressed. Having made such an assumption, you might not want to talk to this person. But instead you could ask: 'How do you feel today; would you like me to get you anything?' By checking out how she feels you could test your own understanding. She might say she feels well and is quite happy, and then ask you to do something for her. This suggests that she cannot be depressed.

Why else would someone look at the floor rather than at you?

Using care values involves getting to understand people – not acting on unchecked assumptions. Non-verbal messages should never be relied on; they should always be checked.

Prejudice

It is easy for people to begin to believe that their system of speaking and communicating verbally is the right one. People who are different can then become stereotyped or labelled as being stupid, difficult or in some way defective because they are different. Stereotyping and labelling people results from a prejudiced view that our way is the only right way.

Where prejudice exists it will obviously create a major barrier to communication but other words and non-verbal communication are likely to be misunderstood and misinterpreted.

A willingness to value difference and to explore what another person means is vital if we are to overcome prejudice.

Think it over...

Many years ago an adolescent girl was interviewed by a psychiatrist. The psychiatrist asked what the girl hoped for in the future. The girl responded by saying that she hoped to get married and live in a banjo. 'But a banjo is a musical instrument,' replied the psychiatrist. 'Yes, I know that' replied the girl, 'but many of my friends live in banjos and I think that's much better than living in an ordinary street'. The psychiatrist is said to have concluded that the girl had a mental disorder.

The psychiatrist did not know that in the local area the term 'banjo' was used to mean a no-through road with a turning circle at the end.

How can you prevent misunderstandings such as the misunderstanding in the story above by using your communication skills?

Lack of confidence

It is vitally important to have the ability to check assumptions and to be prepared to learn when involved in communication work with other people. Overconfidence can lead to our making inappropriate assumptions about people. The opposite, a lack of confidence, might have a positive outcome if it results in people being prepared to listen, ask questions and learn.

Sometimes a lack of experience can create a sense of threat, however, and a care worker or practitioner may have a strong emotional desire to withdraw and not to ask appropriate questions or build an understanding of other people. Unless you are actively involved in checking your understanding of another person's communication, communication is likely to go wrong. If a lack of confidence results in a lack of interaction then there is a barrier to overcome.

Most people develop their confidence by mixing with people who are not neighbours, friends or family. If you gradually learn the skill of checking what other people mean you can increase your confidence in communication work.

Hostility

Within health and care work, professional workers sometimes have to communicate with people who are hostile towards them. Sometimes people in health settings become anxious or afraid. Fear can create hatred and hostility that can be focused on health care workers. Social workers also encounter people who are afraid that their lifestyle will be criticised or judged. Sometimes bad reports about hospital or care services make people suspicious of care staff.

If you are faced by people who are angry or hostile it will be important to stay calm and to use good listening skills in order to try to build a sense of trust with the angry person. It is quite difficult to follow this advice, because you have to be able to control your own emotions and this is a skill that can take time to learn. See the section on coping with angry behaviour on page 27.

2.4 Communication when working in teams

Communication in teams may be about sharing information and/or it might be about developing the relationships between people.

Bales (1970) put forward a theory of task and maintenance activity within groups, such as teams found within health and social care. Teams may have to transmit the following information:

* details of events that have happened while staff have been on duty need to be 'handed over' to new staff that are just coming on duty. This activity is usually called a 'hand over'

* details of the service user plan. When a service user goes into a care home there will be a care plan based on the initial assessment of the service user's need. Staff usually need to know the details of this assessment. In addition staff need to update their knowledge of individual service user's needs

* staff may need to transmit information about policies and procedures to ensure that everybody is up to date with the organisation's policy.

Transmitting this information would form the task of a staff team group discussion. But working together in a team is a social activity. People cannot just concentrate on their work as if they were machines. People need to feel that they belong and that other people in the group respect them. Relationship work might include:

* using humour to defuse tension and conflict

* discussing individual thoughts and feelings about training needs and the development of caring skills

* providing emotional support and encouragement for members of the team.

Bales argued that there needs to be a balance between the practical work of achieving a task and the social needs of group members. Bales (1970) suggested that observers could understand and analyse what was happening in a group by using an interaction analysis of individual members' behaviour. Such an analysis might enable the observer to understand how a group was moving between the focus on task activity and a focus on social activity. An interaction analysis involves classifying the way people behave using defined categories. Bales's categories are outlined in Table 2.1.

BALES'S CATEGORIES	
Group task (including transmission of information)	* Gives suggestion (including taking the lead) * Gives opinion (including feelings and wishes) * Gives information (including clarifying and confirming) * Asks for information * Asks for opinion * Asks for suggestion
Group maintenance (relationship work) (called 'Social-emotional Area' by Bales)	* Seems friendly * Dramatises * Agrees * Disagrees * Shows tension * Seems unfriendly

TABLE 2.1 *Bales's categories*

Using categories can be a useful way of gaining an insight into how an individual is influencing the work and the emotional maintenance or feeling involved in group communication. It is possible to design a grid that can be used minute by minute to try to categorise the task and maintenance behaviours occurring in groups. An example is shown in Table 2.2.

	1	2	3	4	5	6	7	8	9	10
Group task										
Starting discussion										
Giving information										
Asking for information										
Clarifying discussion										
Summarising discussion										
Group maintenance										
Humour										
Expressing group feelings										
Including others										
Being supportive										

TABLE 2.2 *A grid designed for use in categorising the task and maintenance behaviours of individuals in groups*

Think it over...

In a group of five or six people, take four matchsticks each and agree on a topic for group discussion. Next, agree the following rules for the discussion. Only one person may speak at a time. Whenever that person speaks, he or she must place a matchstick on the floor. When people run out of matchsticks they cannot say anything. No one may say anything unless others have finished. Non-verbal communication is allowed. People should not speak for more than one minute.

This exercise should emphasise the importance of group maintenance activity. The matchstick game can make people very focused on the task to the exclusion of much of the social maintenance activity. So being in the group might make you feel awkward or tense.

Relationship work is very important because teams need to develop a sense of belonging that gives the members a 'group feeling'. This could be described as a group identity. In teams people need to:

* know each other and understand each other's feelings

* have a 'feeling of belonging' shared by people in the group

* share a set of beliefs or norms.

How do people get to know each other and develop a sense of belonging, common purpose and norms? Some researchers claim that there is a pattern to the way the communication develops in individual relationships and in group formation.

Tuckman's theory of group development

Tuckman (1965) analysed around 50 studies on group development and concluded that groups of people generally go through a process of development that can be identified as the four stages of Forming, Storming, Norming and Performing (see Figure 2.11). In 1977 Tuckman and Jensen identified a fifth stage of Adjourning in order to describe the process of ending a group.

Tuckman's four stages of group formation

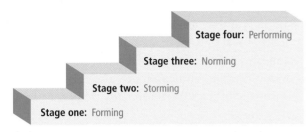

Stage four: Performing
Stage three: Norming
Stage two: Storming
Stage one: Forming

FIGURE 2.11 *Tuckman's four stages*

An explanation of how a group of people comes together to form a team

Forming: when people first get together there is likely to be an introductory stage. People may be unsure about why they are attending a meeting. The purpose of the group may not be clear. People may have little commitment to the group and there may be no clear value system.

Storming: there may be 'power struggles' within the group. Different individuals may contest each other for the leadership of the group. There may be arguments about how the group should work, who should do tasks and so on. Groups can fail at this stage and individuals can decide to drop out because they do not feel comfortable with other people in the group.

Teams might split into sub groups who refuse to communicate with each other, if they become stuck in the storming stage.

Norming: at this stage group members develop a set of common beliefs and values. People are likely to begin to trust each other and develop clear roles. Norms are shared expectations that group members have of each other. Norms enable people to work together as a group.

Performing: because people share the same values and norms the group is able to perform tasks effectively. People may feel that they are comfortable and belong in the group. There may be a sense of high morale.

Adjourning: the group has to conclude their activities and find an acceptable way for group members to part. The group has to complete and end the existence of the group's identity.

> ### Key concept
>
> *Team norms:* for a group to perform effectively, members will need to share a common system of beliefs, values or norms relevant to the purpose of the group. It may be very important to identify the extent to which a team does share a common set of beliefs and norms when observing a team or discussing communication within groups.

2.5 Clients and care settings

Particular communication barriers

Some examples of communication barriers in specific settings are outlined in Table 2.3.

Infants and young children

Infancy is the stage of life before children develop language. Infants communicate with their carers through eye contact and through sounds that later develop into words. Carers usually try to attract the interest of infants through placing their face close to the infant and making eye contact. Most people instinctively talk to infants using a high-pitched voice and it is believed that infants have an in-built tendency to respond to a high-pitched voice with varied voice tone.

When communicating with children it is very important to remember that children do not understand language in the same way that most adults do. Adults and adolescents understand that words are symbols that stand for things. Adults can easily understand that a word like 'wicked' can have many different meanings, but children are likely to have trouble with this idea. If a child has grown up in a family that uses the word 'wicked' to mean 'evil' they may become very upset to be told that they are wearing a wicked T-shirt. When you are only 3–5 years old a word has to have a fixed meaning. If you say something is 'scary' then a young child is likely to understand that you are talking about monsters; children usually do not generalise their understanding of words until they get older.

Children simply do not think the same way as adolescents and adults. If you use leading questions such as 'Do you think it is time to have a drink now?', children will often answer 'Yes', not because they have carefully thought through the issues and come to the considered conclusion that they do want a drink, but because they are used to trusting and wanting to please adults by agreeing with them. It is therefore very easy to 'put words into children's mouths' and get them to say things that they do not really believe in. Care workers may often use leading questions in order to try and guide children into new activities.

Children can be easily frightened by adults who do not appear friendly or supportive, especially if they are tall or 'big' and talking using a loud or fast pattern of speech. It is important to establish a sense of emotional safety before communicating with children – and this principle is also true of working with many other service user groups.

Naturally, children have a much smaller vocabulary than adults and children often do not understand the concepts and words that an adult might use. When communicating with children it is very important to use simple words and phrases that the child may be able to recognise. Some children may not be familiar with very formal communication styles, and it may be important to talk in an informal way that is appropriate to the culture and speech community that the child belongs to.

Some specific skills that you might observe care workers using when they communicate with young children include the following:

∗ care workers may use a different range of voice tone than they might use with adults

∗ care workers may come much closer to young children than they would when interacting with adults

∗ you might see more examples of touch – for instance, holding hands – than you would expect to see in adult interactions. Touch may create a feeling of friendship and safety between a child and familiar carers

∗ care workers are careful to make eye contact when speaking to children; eye contact is sometimes more fixed during a conversation than it might be with adults

∗ care workers might use lots of questions – not really as questions but to guide children – for example, 'shall we leave the sand tray now'.

∗ care workers might be careful to speak softly and constantly change the tone of their voice; this might help to keep children interested in the conversation and help to create a friendly relationship between the worker and the child.

SETTING	BARRIERS
Hospitals	* Staff time may be limited, preventing effective support and understanding * The professional role of medical experts may exclude patients from management of health needs * Technical terminology and formal language may create a barrier to understanding * Staff may make assumptions about lifestyle habits * Emotional distress may create a specific problem for communication
Family home	* Emotional relationships may not be understood by outside people * Individuals may have developed private systems of language and communication * There is the risk of stereotyping or making assumptions about diverse cultures
Day centres	* Staff time and other resource constraints may prevent effective communication and support * Different speech patterns may create a barrier between members * Individuals may make inappropriate assumptions or stereotype people * Emotional distress may create a specific problem for communication
Nursing and residential homes	* Staff time and other resource constraints may prevent effective communication support * Sensory disabilities * Specific disabilities associated with mental health needs * Emotional distress * Person-centred communication approaches for valuing individuals may not be used * Individuals may make inappropriate assumptions or stereotype people
Early years settings	* Staff time and other resource constraints may prevent effective communication support * There is the risk of stereotyping or making assumptions about diverse cultures. * The use of adult speech patterns and non-verbal communication may not be understood by young children * Children will have a limited vocabulary and a different way of understanding concepts compared with adults
Special educational settings	* Staff time and other resource constraints * There is the risk of stereotyping or making assumptions about diverse cultures. * The use of adult speech patterns and non-verbal communication may not be understood * People with a learning difficulty may have a limited vocabulary and different ways of understanding concepts.

TABLE 2.3 *Examples of communication barriers in specific settings*

Talking to children keeps them interested

People with a specific learning difficulty

Specific learning difficulties may include issues such as:

* autism, a disorder involving difficulty in understanding human relationships

* dyslexia (a disturbance in the ability to read and write)

* dysphasia (a disorder of speech).

Autism

People with autism may not produce or understand non-verbal language in the same way that many people are used to. Certain words may have a significance that is hard to understand without getting to know the individual. Care workers who communicate with individuals who have a specific learning difficulty will be very concerned to learn about the individual thought patterns and ways of communicating that the person may be able to develop. Makaton provides a system which is useful for encouraging the development of language and communication skills for people who have a learning difficulty.

Dyslexia

Like many conditions, dyslexia does not result in a simple set of problems. One person's dyslexia may be different from another's. Dyslexia can delay the age at which a child learns to read;

it is also associated with a serious difficulty in spelling words and understanding how letters are arranged to make words. Some people with dyslexia can communicate very effectively using spoken language, and modern information technology can sometimes compensate for the difficulties experienced by those suffering from dyslexia with spelling and writing. Voice-recognition software, for instance, can be used to enable a person with dyslexia to convert speech into writing.

Dysphasia

When people have a disturbance with their use of language this disability is called dysphasia. People who have had a stroke often have difficulty in saying certain words. Sometimes people with dysphasia become distressed because they cannot speak clearly. If you are communicating with a dysphasic person it is important to be calm and patient; sometimes you may be able to guess a word the person is struggling with and the individual may nod to indicate that you are correct. People with dysphasia are likely to become tired and stressed if they feel that they are expected to communicate verbally for any length of time.

Learning difficulty

People with learning difficulty may have a limited vocabulary (range of words that they can use) and may sometimes use words or phrases in a way that is difficult to understand without knowing about their lives and preferences. As with many other communication difficulties it is important to understand as much as possible about the person you are working with in order to understand his or her speech, and to make them feel at ease and comfortable.

With respect to general learning difficulty, current practice emphasises the importance of person-centred care. It is vitally important for care workers to learn about the individual needs and preferences of the people that they work with. The skill of active listening and asking skilled questions is therefore a very important skill when working with adult service users.

Speech disability

If you are communicating with someone with a speech disability it is important to be calm and patient and to learn as much as possible about the person's use of sound to help you understand their words.

> **Key concept**
>
> *Person-centred care:* care that places 'the person' at the centre of decision-making and activities. Person-centred care is care that seeks to value the individual 'personhood' of service users.

In services for people with learning difficulty, the government White Paper 'Valuing People' (2001) argues that services should use person-centred approaches when planning care. 'Person-centred' means that care must be focused on the specific needs and wishes of the service user. Service users plan their own life and make their own choices using help from family, friends and professionals. Service users are empowered to control their own life; their life is not controlled by the wishes of other people.

People with sensory, speech or other communication impairments

Visual impairment

People with a visual impairment will not be able to interpret your body language. Because of this, it may be important to use words to describe things that a sighted person may take for granted. You may also be able to explain your feelings through voice tone. This might include how you feel about an issue; for example, it might be obvious to someone who can see your face that you feel sad, but you might need to put your emotions into words so that a person with a visual disability can understand you. Touch may also be important; some registered blind people can work out what you look like if they can touch your face in order to build an understanding of your features. You can often explain how you feel using touch, but it is important to be sure that a service user is comfortable with being touched. You must never take it for granted that a person

with low vision would expect to be touched even on the hands or arms.

Hearing impairment

People with a hearing impairment may be able to use a hearing aid in order to increase the volume of sound that they can sense. One problem with hearing aids is that they often increase the volume of background noise as well as the volume of a person's voice. Some people with a hearing disability use partial lip-reading in order to understand what a person is saying. It does make sense for a person to say, 'I'm sorry I can't hear you, I need to put my glasses on.' It is very important that a person with a hearing disability can see your face, read your body language and watch your lips.

Hayman (1998) notes the following points for communicating with people who have hearing impairments:

* make sure the person can see you clearly
* face both the light and the person at all times
* include the person in your conversation
* do not obscure your mouth
* speak clearly and slowly. Repeat if necessary, but you may need to rephrase your words
* do not shout into a person's ear or hearing aid
* minimise background noise
* use your eyes, facial expressions and hand gestures, where appropriate.

People who are born Deaf often learn to use British Sign Language; this is a different language to English and is not a set of signs for English words. The ability to use some signs in BSL will enable care workers to communicate with members of the 'Deaf community' in the UK.

Some people have difficulty making the sounds that we expect to hear in relation to words. Speech therapists provide a service that may help people to develop their ability to communicate more effectively using speech. As with all disabilities, getting to know the individual person and creating a safe and supportive atmosphere will be central to improving your ability to communicate with a person who has a speech impairment.

People with disabilities – the risk of stereotyping

People with mobility disabilities can usually communicate in exactly the same way as mobile people. However people with disabilities are often stereotyped as being 'defective people'; in other words a person who needs a wheelchair to get around is seen as somebody who is not competent to express their own thoughts and feelings. The classic way of understanding this stereotype is the 'does he take sugar?' situation.

A service user is wheeled into a tea room by a carer, and the person serving the tea communicates only with the carer. Why ask the person in the wheelchair if they take sugar? The person serving the tea has assured that a person who needs a carer is a 'non-person' incapable of communicating choices!

'Does he take sugar?'

FIGURE 2.12 *A disability does not mean an inability to communicate*

Disabled people are at risk of being patronised and sometimes being talked to as if they were children. It is possible that some people only understand caring as something you do with children. Because of this there is an assumption or stereotype that anybody who needs care must be childlike. There is, therefore, the risk that people will automatically use more fixed eye contact, a higher tone of voice and simple language with anybody who has a carer. Many people with coordination or mobility problems are vulnerable to the assumptions of other people. You may be, for example, an expert on astrophysics but people will attempt to communicate with you as if you were only five years old.

As with all interpersonal communication it is vital to get to know the individual needs, preferences and abilities of the individuals that you work with. Active listening provides a central tool for achieving this goal.

People attending an accident and emergency unit – working with distressed people

People and their relatives in an accident and emergency unit are likely to experience stress and perhaps distress. It will usually be important to use calming skills in order to help communicate effectively with people who are stressed. There is always the possibility that people who are stressed or in a state of distress may become aggressive or hostile. Aggression is an issue that can occur in many health and care settings; it involves some important communication skills, and these skills might be particularly useful in coping with people who experience distress

Preventing aggression

One of the key ways of showing respect for other people is to be assertive. The word 'assertion' is often misunderstood. Many people see assertion as 'sticking up for yourself', but being assertive involves much more than this. Being assertive is about remaining calm, and showing respect and value for other people. Assertion involves being clear about your own needs and intentions and being able to communicate in a clear, controlled and calm manner.

Fear and aggression are two of the basic emotions that we experience. It is easy to give in to our basic emotions and become either submissive or aggressive when we feel stressed. Assertion is an alternative way of coping that involves controlling the basic emotions involved in running away or fighting. Assertion involves a mental attitude of trying to **negotiate**, trying to solve problems rather than giving in to emotional impulses.

Assertion is different from both submission and aggression, Assertion involves being able to negotiate a solution to a problem.

Winning and losing

During an argument aggressive people might demand that they are right and other people are wrong. They will want to win while others lose. The opposite of aggression is to be weak or submissive. Submissive people accept that they

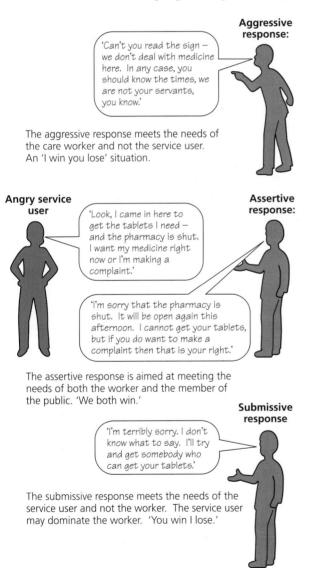

Aggressive response:

'Can't you read the sign – we don't deal with medicine here. In any case, you should know the times, we are not your servants, you know.'

The aggressive response meets the needs of the care worker and not the service user. An 'I win you lose' situation.

Angry service user

'Look, I came in here to get the tablets I need – and the pharmacy is shut. I want my medicine right now or I'm making a complaint.'

Assertive response:

'I'm sorry that the pharmacy is shut. It will be open again this afternoon. I cannot get your tablets, but if you do want to make a complaint then that is your right.'

The assertive response is aimed at meeting the needs of both the worker and the member of the public. 'We both win.'

Submissive response

'I'm terribly sorry. I don't know what to say. I'll try and get somebody who can get your tablets.'

The submissive response meets the needs of the service user and not the worker. The service user may dominate the worker. 'You win I lose.'

FIGURE 2.13 *How assertion enables both people to win*

will lose, get told off, or be put down. Assertive behaviour is different from both of these responses. In an argument an assertive person will try to reach an answer where no one has to lose or be 'put down'. Assertion is a skill where 'win-win' situations can happen – no one has to be the loser. For example, consider the following scenario in which a member of the public is angry because of being unable to get some tablets (see Figure 2.13).

Assertion can help care staff to cope with difficult and challenging situations.

To be assertive a person usually has to:

* understand the situation that they he or she is in – including facts, details and other people's perceptions

* be able to control personal emotions and stay calm

* be able to act assertively using the right body language

* be able to act assertively using the right words and statements.

Table 2.4 compares some of the different characteristics commonly associated with assertion, submission and aggression.

If you behave assertively, your calm, respectful behaviour may help to prevent aggression in other people. This is because you will not 'set yourself up as a target' for other people's emotions. If you lose control of your own emotions and become angry you may increase the threat experienced by another person. They may feel emotionally justified in abusing or even physically attacking you – because 'attack is the best defence'. If you appear weak and afraid you may invite abuse and attack because this may increase the frustration experienced by another person. A person who is weak and afraid my also appear to be an easy target – easy to dominate and control. If you listen and show respect for another person you may create an emotional environment in which that individual feels encouraged to respond with listening and respect.

Coping with aggression

Anger is a powerful emotion and it often looks as though people suddenly lose their temper

SUBMISSIVE BEHAVIOUR INVOLVES:	ASSERTIVE BEHAVIOUR INVOLVES:	AGGRESSIVE BEHAVIOUR INVOLVES:
Main emotion: fear	Main emotion: confidence	Main emotion: anger
Letting other people win	Negotiating so that everyone wins	Wanting to win
Understanding and acceptance only of other people's needs	Understanding and accepting your own and other people's needs	Understanding only your own needs
A mental attitude that other people are more important than you	A mental attitude that it is important to negotiate in order to get the best outcome for yourself and others	A mental attitude that you are more important than other people
Not speaking or only asking questions to find out what is wanted	Listening carefully	Not listening to others – making demands
Lack of respect for self	Respect for self and others	Lack of respect for others
Speaking quietly	Speaking in a clear calm voice	Shouting or talking loudly
Submissive body language including: ∗ looking down ∗ not looking at others ∗ looking frightened ∗ looking tense.	Relaxed body language including: ∗ varied eye contact ∗ looking confident ∗ keeping hands and arms at your side.	Threatening body language including: ∗ fixed eye contact ∗ tense muscles ∗ waving or folding arms ∗ clenching fingers.

TABLE 2.4 *Characteristics commonly associated with assertion, submission and aggression*

without a justified reason. A service user might suddenly start shouting or start making abusive comments. In many situations, this service user might have felt stressed long before the outburst of anger. Frustration and tension can grow as individuals fail to control their own emotions and their circumstances.

Triggers

As tension mounts, it may only take a single remark or some little thing that has gone wrong, to push the person into an angry outburst. People who feel stressed may only need a trigger incident to set off an explosion of anger that has built up inside them.

After an explosion of anger, stressed people can still feel tense. Very often they may feel that is someone else's fault that they have been made to feel so angry. Anger can flare up again if the person is not given respect and encouraged to become calm. As time passes, tension may reduce as stress and levels of high emotional arousal decrease.

Not all angry outbursts follow this pattern. Some people learn to use aggression to get their way and some people can switch aggressive emotions on and off as they wish. Being angry can sometimes be a reaction that a person has chosen. But it is wrong to assume that most outbursts of aggression and anger are deliberate. A great deal of aggression experienced by care

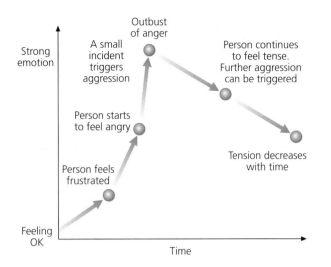

FIGURE 2.14 *Stages in the development of aggression*

workers will be an emotional response to frustration or distress.

The desire to fight or run

When people are aggressive or abusive they may make care workers feel threatened. The simple in-built emotional response to threat is to want to run or fight. An unskilled response to aggression is to be aggressive back. This will almost certainly escalate into a conflict situation, which is unlikely to have a positive outcome.

Even in mildly aggressive encounters one or both people are likely to feel resentment towards each other following the incident. A professional skilled response is to stay calm, be assertive rather than aggressive, calm the other person, and resolve the situation without creating resentment.

Care workers are unlikely to be able to switch off feelings of being threatened simply by wishing them away. Usually, workers will switch off the threat using positive thoughts about their own past experiences, their skills in being able to calm people, or just by using their own professional role to protect themselves from feeling 'got at'. If care workers can think 'this person is distressed because of his or her situation', rather than 'this person is out to get me' they may be able to switch off the emotions that create the feeling of being threatened.

Staying calm

Being calm depends on the thoughts that we

have, but it is also a practical skill which can be acted out and rehearsed. If care workers can appear to be calm their own behaviour may have

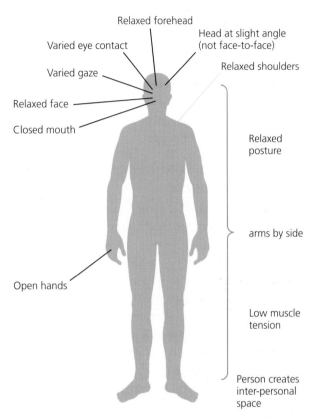

FIGURE 2.15 *Non-verbal signs of being calm*

a calming effect on others. Non-verbal signs of being calm are summarised in Figure 2.15.

It is important to remember to breathe gently and slowly. Slow, careful breathing can help to create relaxation and calmness as well as looking calm to others. Sometimes it is appropriate that body posture should be at a slight angle towards an angry person. A face-to-face posture is sometimes interpreted as an attempt to dominate or be threatening. The volume of speech should not be raised, it is important to talk in a normal tone and volume and to display that you do not feel threatened or angry.

Communicating respect and value

It is important to acknowledge the feelings and complaints that distressed people may be experiencing. If the other person feels that he or she is being taken seriously and is being listened to, this may have a calming effect. Active listening skills and the ability to keep the conversation going will be very important. A professional conversation should be warm and sincere while also seeking to build an understanding of the situation. Thanking a person for clarifying issues may be one way in which a worker can reduce the frustration that another person may feel. If a worker can communicate an understanding of the other person's point of view this may go a long way toward calming a situation and preventing further outbreaks of anger.

Creating trust and negotiating with distressed people

If you can successfully calm an angry or distressed person, the next step will be to try and establish a sense of common ground or liking between each other. It is at this stage that a skilled worker will attempt to build an understanding of the other person's viewpoint. Creating trust involves meeting the other person's self-esteem needs. In some situations it may be necessary to make the other person feel important. Sometimes it may be appropriate to say just a little about your own feelings, background, and so on, if this helps to build bridges and create a sense of safety with the other person. It is usually appropriate to convey that you are open-minded and supportive, but it is important that you do not agree with everything that the other person demands. It will be important to keep the conversation going and to keep the other person talking – perhaps using questioning and active listening skills.

Once you have built a level of understanding with a distressed person, it may then be possible to try and sort things out and to negotiate what kind of help or support you can offer. At this stage in the interaction it may be possible to take a problem-solving approach. Problem solving may start off by clarifying the issues that are involved and exploring alternative solutions.

Sometimes it may be necessary to structure expectations. This means gently introducing ideas of what is and is not possible. It is important not to argue with a distressed person, as arguing may only force him or her back into being aggressive or withdrawn. If you have to say 'no' to a demand, it may often be better to slowly lead up

to the expectation that you will say no, rather than directly confronting a person with a 'stone wall' rejection of their views. For instance, 'I understand what you're saying and I'll see what I can do, but it would be wrong to promise anything', or 'We can try, but I am not hopeful'.

Only after you have developed a sense of trust and friendliness with the distressed person should you try to resolve the issues involved in the aggressive incident. During this stage of negotiation it may be important to bring factual information into the conversation. It is important not to appear patronising when offering information. It is also important to clearly explain technical information that the other person may not fully understand.

Sometimes it may not be possible to reach agreement with a distressed person, and in these circumstances it is important to conclude the conversation, leaving a positive emotional outcome, even if agreement has not been reached. It may be possible to agree to resume a conversation tomorrow, or to thank the person for his or her time and offer to talk again. It will always be important to leave the person with an increased sense of self-esteem even if he or she did not agree with your viewpoint.

While you cannot always give other people what they want, you can always give respect and a little time in supportive communication. Listening and respect may go some way to creating a positive emotional environment. Steps to take in order to manage a conversation with an angry person are shown in Figure 2.16.

Real conversations do not always follow simple stages but it is important not to attempt to negotiate and solve problems before listening and building trust.

People resident in a hospital ward – providing emotional support

As with many health care settings, people within a hospital ward may experience distress and it is important to provide emotional support. You can use active listening skills in order to build an understanding of people receiving medical care. Good listening skills and supportive body language can lead to effective emotional support.

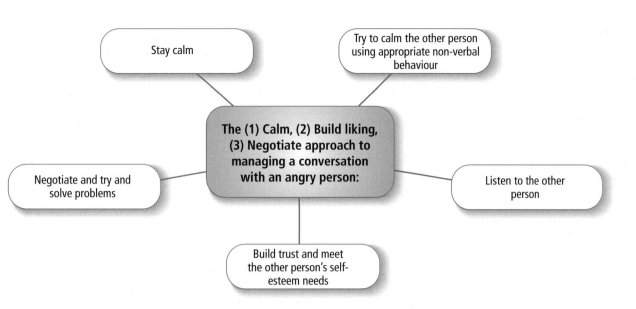

FIGURE 2.16 *Managing a conversation with an angry person*

Emotional support

Supportive body language involves looking friendly. When meeting a person it is usually appropriate to smile, to express interest through eye contact and to maintain a relaxed posture – free of muscle tension – which indicates a readiness to talk and listen. It is difficult to define a simple set of rules for supportive body language because each individual will have their own expectations about what is appropriate and normal. The most important thing about supportive body language is to learn to monitor the effects that our behaviour is having on the other person. Being supportive involves being aware of your own non-verbal behaviour and monitoring how your non-verbal behaviour is affecting others.

It is important for service users to feel emotionally safe and able to share experiences. The skills for creating a sense of emotional safety were first identified by Carl Rogers (1902–1987). Originally, these skills were seen as a basis for counselling relationships, but they have since become adopted as a basis for any befriending or supportive communication. There are three conditions for a supportive conversation and these are that the carer must show (or convey) a sense of warmth, understanding and sincerity to the other person. These conditions sometimes have other names:

* warmth (sometimes called acceptance)
* understanding (originally called empathy)
* sincerity (originally called genuineness).

Warmth

Warmth means being perceived as a friendly, accepting person. In order to influence another person to view you this way you will need to demonstrate that you do not stereotype and label others. You will need to show that you do not judge other people's lifestyles as good or bad, right or wrong. This is sometimes referred to as a non-judgemental attitude.

Conveying warmth means being willing to listen to others. It means having the ability to prove that you are listening to a person because you can remember what they have said to you. Warmth involves using active listening. That is, you give your attention to individuals when they talk, and remember what they say. You can then reflect their words back again.

In the scenario in Figure 2.17, the nurse is able to show the patient that she is listening by repeating some of the things that he has said. The repetition is not 'parrot fashion'; the nurse has used her own way of speaking. The nurse has also avoided being judgemental. When the patient said that no one cared, the nurse did not argue with him. Warmth makes it safe for the

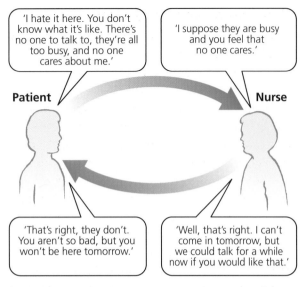

FIGURE 2.17 *developing a supportive sense of warmth involves being non-judgemental*

patient to express his feelings. Warmth means that the nurse could disagree with what a patient has said, but the patient needs to feel safe that he will not be put down.

In developing the skill of showing warmth, it is important not to judge. Carers should accept that people have the right to be the way they are, and to make their own choices. While you may disapprove of someone's behaviour, you must show that you do not dislike them as a person.

Key concept

Understanding means learning about the individual identity and beliefs that a person has. Carl Rogers saw the idea of understanding or empathy as the ability to experience another person's world as if it was your own world. The key part being the 'as if'. We always understand our own world and we know that other people have different experiences from our own. It is important to try to really understand others' thoughts and feelings.

Active listening provides a useful tool that enables staff to learn about people. If a person is listened to, he or she may experience a feeling of being understood. If a care worker is warm and non-judgemental, it becomes safe for a service user to talk about his or her life. If the care worker checks that he or she understands the person, this may result in the service user feeling valued. As the person feels that they are valued, so he or she may talk more. The more the person talks, the more the care worker has a chance to learn about that service user.

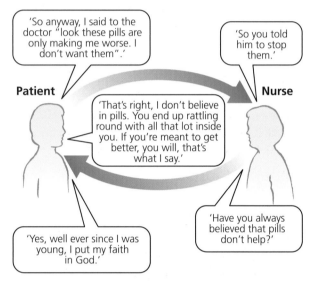

FIGURE 2.18 *developing a supportive sense of understanding involves active listening*

By listening and conveying warmth the health care worker is being given the privilege of learning about the patient's religious views. Understanding can grow from a conversation that conveys value for the other person. A sense of trust may develop out of a sense of understanding. If you feel you are understood then you may feel it is safe to share your thoughts and worries.

Sincerity

Being sincere means being yourself – honest and real. It means not acting, not using set phrases or professional styles, which are not really you. Being real has to involve being non-judgemental though – trying to understand people, rather than trying to give people advice. If being honest means giving other people your advice, don't do it! However, when you listen and learn about other people, do use your own normal language.

Patient 'But what's the point in talking to you? I mean, you don't really care, it's just your job.'

Nurse 'It is my job, but I do care about you, and I would be pleased to talk with you. I chose this work because I care and because I can make the time to listen if you want to talk about it.'

Learning to create a supportive relationship with people involves practice and a great deal of reflection. A care worker may be able to tell if his or her communication is effective because the other person may reflect his or her behaviour. This means, if you are warm and understanding you may find that others are warm and friendly towards you. If you are honest and sincere, people may be honest and sincere with you in return. The quality of a supportive relationship becomes a two-way process.

Think it over – developing supportive skills

You could try the following ideas for developing your supportive communication skills.

1. Work with a friend. Take turns in imagining that you are upset or sad whilst the other person uses reflective listening skills. Tape-record the conversation. Play the tape back and evaluate your performance in terms of warmth, understanding and sincerity.

2. Watch videos of conversational skills or counselling situations where warmth, understanding and sincerity are demonstrated. Discuss how this is effective and how you might develop your own conversational skills.

3. Think about your own conversations with service users – keep a logbook to reflect on your own skills development.

4. Write up examples of being warm, understanding and sincere. Discuss your examples with your tutor and ask for feedback.

Creating a caring presence

Verbal conversational skills are very important in enabling people to feel supported, but part of what is needed may simply be to provide a 'caring presence'. Sometimes just sitting with someone – simply being with a person because you care about that individual – creates a sense of being valued and supported. Engebretson (2004) explains this sense of being valued and supported without words as the creation of a caring presence. She explains the importance of being open to the experience of other people. Health and care work cannot simply be about 'doing things' to people. Creating a caring presence is about sharing an understanding of the feelings that service users have. Engebretson explains how nurses can work on an emotional level in order to make a real difference to what people experience when they receive health care.

People in consultation with a medical practitioner

The term 'patient' has been around for many centuries and the idea is that the people needing help are patient while the expert medical practitioner works on them. Many people who consult medical practitioners expect to be passive and expect simple pharmaceutical (to be given a tablet) solutions to their problem. Half a century ago a visit to the doctor would involve patients explaining their problem and accepting the advice received in return. The term 'doctor's orders' was sometimes used to describe the treatment plan that a patient had to follow. Patients often thought of doctors as being senior people who were entitled to give orders – rather like officers in the army.

Some patients and some medical practitioners may find this idea of giving and receiving orders a satisfying prospect. But there are problems with communications that assume this kind of power relationship.

Many people's health problems are associated with economic and lifestyle issues. For example, some people develop health problems associated with being overweight or with smoking. Just giving people information or orders to eat less and exercise more, or to stop smoking is almost wholly ineffective in helping patients. There is no simple tablet or procedure that enables people to change their lifestyle. In order for 'the patients' to become healthier they must stop being patient, and instead become actively involved in their own health issues.

In order to encourage active involvement, consultations may need to involve a more empowering approach where the patients take responsibility for understanding and managing their needs – in partnership with a health professional – rather than delegating total responsibility for treatment to health staff.

Medical practitioners should communicate their knowledge to service users and enable service users to make their own decisions and choices about care plans or medical treatment. Empowering communication is communication that aims to give service users choice and control of the service that they receive.

> ### Key concept
>
> *Empowerment:* this enables service users to make choices and take control of their own life. Empowerment involves patients taking some responsibility for the management of their health needs.

An example of empowerment

In 2001 the government launched the 'Expert Patient Initiative'. The idea of an 'expert patient' is that a person with a long-term, or chronic, illness such as arthritis can learn to take control of the management of his or her condition. Expert medical staff can provide advice and guidance, but the patient is the expert on his or her own body. Thus patients work in partnership with medical staff in order to build their own treatment plan.

The 'expert patient' is empowered to take control of his or her own medical condition. The expert patient does not simply have to comply with the treatment prescribed.

Getting empowerment to take place

There are pressures that may limit the degree to which service users are empowered.

∗ some care workers may enjoy a sense of prestige and power that might come from making decisions for other people. In reality, some care staff may be reluctant to share their expert status

∗ lack of time may represent a problem for some care workers. Working in partnership may require longer conversations than a more directive approach

∗ some service users may resist 'working in partnership'. Some service users may find it preferable to delegate responsibility for meeting their needs to others. Taking responsibility for your own life may require a well-organised self-concept, a degree of confidence in your own abilities and perhaps some energy and enthusiasm for being in control. Many vulnerable people may initially prefer 'to be looked after' by professionals.

Christine Descombes (2004) provides evidence that within medical practice, 'It is still the doctor who controls the whole patient-practitioner encounter. It is the doctor who decides just what information will be given and how much use can be made of it' (2000: 94). Establishing an empowering approach will require much more than simply giving clear information to service users.

Older people

As with all adult service user groups, it will be vitally important that care workers are skilled in using active listening and supportive skills. The section on supportive skills and caring presence related to residents in hospitals is equally important when working with older people.

There are special problems that may arise when working with people who are disorientated or who have memory problems. A 90-year-old service user might say, for example, 'My mother visited me yesterday.' On the surface, such a statement appears to be irrational. From a care perspective it is very important not to challenge the irrationality of what is being said. The most important thing is to make the older person feel valued and respected. People with memory disorders, often substitute inappropriate words. The person has said that her mother visited and perhaps the care worker knows that the visitor was, in fact, a daughter. The service user has simply used an incorrect word, although she knew what she meant; perhaps, too, the care worker knew what the service user meant. The technical inaccuracy is not important. It is much more important that the service user feels safe and respected.

Sometimes disorientated service users may make statements about needing to go to work or to go home to look after their children. Once again, it is important not to argue, but rather to try and divert the conversation in a way that values the person, as is illustrated in the following scenario.

Active listening skills are important for care workers

Care workers often develop the skills of managing a conversation in a way that demonstrates respect and value and prevents aggression. The conversation below takes place in a care home for older people and illustrates how difficult encounters can sometimes be resolved by taking an assertive approach that also seeks to value others.

Relative: What have you done to my mother? She's so much worse than before. You aren't looking after her properly. She can't eat because of the rubbish food you give out.

Worker: Your mother does look worse today. Perhaps you would like to sit down and we can talk.

Relative: Well, you tell me what is going on, then, and why the food is such rubbish!

Worker: I'll explain what we're doing if you like, and I'm sorry that your mother doesn't like the food. Could you tell me what sort of things she really does like to eat?

Relative: Not the rubbish here.

Worker: Sometimes it's possible to increase someone's appetite by just offering a very small tasty piece of something that person really likes, perhaps fruit or a tiny piece of bread and jam?

SCENARIO

Service user: I must go home and get the tea ready for my children.

Care worker: All right. Shall we walk to your room then – you might want your coat?

Service user: Yes, that's right, you are so kind.

Care worker: [now in service user's room] Is this photograph a photograph of your son and daughter?

Service user: Yes, that's right.

Care worker: They've both got married now. Haven't they both grown up?

Service user: Yes, I'm very proud of them. They're coming to visit me tomorrow.

Care worker: That's wonderful. Why don't we go downstairs and have a cup of tea?

Service user Yes, that would be very nice. You are so kind to me.

In this script, the carer has avoided arguing about logic, and instead the carer has gently helped the service user to remember the age of her children now. Throughout the conversation, the carer has shown respect and value for the service user.

Relative: What, and you are going to sort that out, are you!

Worker: I've found that it works for a lot of people. But can you give me some ideas of what your mother would like?

Relative: Well she likes pears and cherry jam, but good stuff – not like here.

Worker: OK, could you possibly bring some of her favourite things in and we could try and see if that would help.

Relative: Why should I?

Worker: Well, it might help. Everyone is different and you are the person who would really know what your mother is likely to enjoy.

Relative: Can't you do something about the food here?

Worker: I'm afraid that the choice of food is limited, but we might be able to work together to improve your mother's appetite as a first step to making things better.

Relative: I suppose it's not up to you to change the food. I'll bring the jam in, but I still think it's not right.

Worker: I'm sorry that you're not happy about the food, but perhaps we can talk again tomorrow.

Relative: Well, thank you for your time – at least I could talk to you.

Discussion

This conversation starts with the relative in an angry mood. The worker responds by remaining assertive and not arguing, or going straight into discussing the complaints that the relative has raised. Instead, the worker attempts to calm the situation and invites the relative to sit down. By inviting the relative to sit down the worker is taking control of the conversation and creating a situation where he or she can use his or her listening skills.

At several points the angry relative is still challenging the worker with complaints and aggressive statements. The worker is careful not to respond to these challenges and risk triggering more aggression. The worker is able to stay calm and to build a sense of trust by keeping the conversation going. The worker is able to ask the relative questions about his mother's needs. The worker is also able to meet the relative's self-esteem needs by pointing out that he is the person who would really know what his mother likes and dislikes.

In this conversation the worker negotiates that the relative will bring some food in. The worker structures the relative's expectations by mentioning the limited choice of food. Because the relative has been listened to, he is willing to stop complaining. He compliments the worker with the statement that at least she listened.

The conversation ends on a positive emotional note, even though the problems of catering in this care setting have not been resolved. The point of this conversation was to meet the emotional needs of the distressed relative and not to find technical solutions to catering problems!

2.6 Giving a talk

Whilst some people feel quite comfortable with the idea of giving a talk, others are filled with emotions that range from nervousness to fear. If you are one of those for whom giving a talk is a daunting prospect, be reassured that many people feel this way. However, there are a number of things that can be done to make it likely that the talk will be a success, and one of these is to prepare adequately for the event. The planning process described in this section, if followed carefully, will increase your chances of giving an interesting presentation in a confident manner. There are also a few tips for dealing with pre-talk nerves.

Remember, too, that it is quite normal, and indeed desirable, to be nervous before making a presentation. As someone once said, 'It's OK to have butterflies in your stomach – you just have to make sure that they fly in the same direction!' The steps described in this section will help to make sure that your butterflies behave themselves.

Being a little nervous may actually improve your presentation

Identifying a topic

Fairly early on in your studies for this unit, you should identify a type of service user and a care setting as the subject for the presentation. You might, for example, choose to consider an aspect of communication with an older person who lives in a residential setting. Alternatively, you may be interested in communication with younger children, perhaps in an early years centre. People with learning disabilities have specific communication needs, as do people with sensory disabilities. If you are able to visit a centre or unit attended by people with the kinds of need you are interested in, this will help you tremendously in preparing and researching your talk.

Remember that the talk is only to last about 5–10 minutes. It will be important to select a topic that can be dealt with adequately in that relatively short time span. For example, it would be hard to explain to people how to use British Sign Language (BSL) in ten minutes. It would be more realistic to explain to people why it can be useful for a hearing person to know BSL, or to point out the kinds of situation where BSL makes a difference (e.g. in theatres, law courts, etc.).

One way to find a good topic is to focus on a particular event, and the learning points that arise from it. In this section, the progress of a typical A-level student, Natalie, is followed as she works on her presentation for this unit.

Natalie is interested in communication issues for people with learning disabilities, and her tutor has arranged for her to visit a day unit run by the local social services department. At the day unit she meets Ellen, a young woman who is about to take part in a facilitated session led by a staff member. Like many people with a learning disability, Ellen is not used to being asked to say what she wants, and usually gives answers that she thinks the staff wants to hear. She also has a limited knowledge of what kinds of things are available to her.

Learning about what's available

At Ellen's day unit, Person Centred Planning has just been introduced by social services, and staff have come up with a way of finding out what each service user wants. One of the workers had been on a special training course to learn how to lead groups to do this, and there is now a weekly meeting at the unit in which people are helped to discover what they like.

This week, the subject is 'fruit'. Staff have brought in a very wide range of fruits for everyone to try. As each fruit is tasted, service users explain their reaction to it by pointing to a face-symbol: a smiley face for 'love it', a grumpy face for 'don't like it', and so on.

Ellen discovers that she loves fresh pineapple, something she has never tasted before, but she is not very keen on kiwi fruit.

Natalie is fascinated by what has happened, and the way it was done. The meeting was led by a **facilitator**, who had been specially trained to help people with learning disabilities to express themselves, asking the right questions, and adapting her listening style to suit the needs of each person. Sometimes, this can be as simple (and as complex) as learning to observe (and correctly interpret) the non-verbal signals that a person gives.

Key concept

Facilitator: a person who helps to make something happen. This is often associated with decision-making or planning.

Natalie has also been introduced to the concept of **Person Centred Planning**. The staff at the unit give her some information about this, but she realises that now she will have to go away and do some more research. How she did this is described in the next section.

Collecting information

Natalie does some Internet research to find out more about Person Centred Planning. She discovers that it was introduced for people with learning disabilities by a government initiative called Valuing People, which was launched in 2001.

Key concept

Person Centred Planning 'A process for continual listening and learning, focused on what is important for someone now and in the future, and acting upon this in alliance with family and friends.'

Source: *Planning With People: Guidance for Implementation Groups* (Department of Health, 2002), p. 12.

Natalie's search reveals several websites with further information about how Person Centred Planning may be carried out, including the Valuing People website, People First and the website for In Control. (Further details of these sites, which have a lot of information about communicating with people with learning disabilities, and empowering them to say what they want, may be found at www.heinemann.co.uk/hotlinks (express code 1562P).)

Besides finding out more about facilitation, Natalie also comes across the concepts of **advocacy**, **self-advocacy** and **self-directed support**.

Key concepts

Advocacy: the act of speaking on behalf of someone else, to make sure that his or her views and wishes are heard.

Self-advocacy: the act of speaking up for yourself.

Self-directed support: a process that involves the service user playing a key role in decision-making about the services he or she wants.

Natalie also spends some time at her local library, to find out more about communicating with people with learning disabilities. By combining what she learnt from her visit to the day unit with Internet and printed information, she finally decides on a topic for her talk (in discussion with her tutor). She decides to call the presentation 'Finding out what people with learning disabilities want'.

Planning your talk

There are a number of factors that Natalie will have to consider when preparing a presentation. These are set out in Table 2.5.

Who are my audience?

Doing an analysis of your audience in advance of giving the talk is essential. Who they are, what they will expect and how many of them there will be are all factors that will have an effect on what you say and how you say it. Social workers, for example, may be very interested in a talk that includes lots of theoretical material, whereas parents or carers may want to hear more about practical issues.

Similarly, the size of the group will also have a bearing on the kind of talk you give. Group size has implications both for the venue that you will need (size of the room, need for a microphone, etc.) and also for the possibility of interaction between speaker and audience. The atmosphere is more likely to be relaxed with a small group and, therefore, people may be more willing to ask

questions. If audience participation is a key element of your presentation, the size of the group may be critical.

A more detailed checklist of aspects of the venue is given at the end of this section (p. 90). At this stage, you should have the following broad considerations in mind.

Natalie will be giving her talk to a group of fellow students. There will be nine people, plus her tutor. She feels that it would be useful for her talk to include both theoretical and practical aspects of communication. She is the only person studying people with learning disabilities for this unit, so she wants to take the opportunity to share some of the key issues with her colleagues.

When will the presentation take place?

Besides forming a clear picture of who your audience is going to be, it is important to find out what time of day you will be giving your talk, and how it fits in with other activities that may be scheduled to take place.

PLANNING A TALK		
Checklist		Notes
Who?	– Who is my target audience? – What are their expectations? – What is the size of the group?	
When?	– When will the talk take place? – What time of day? – What is happening before and after my talk?	
Where?	–– Where will the talk take place? – Will I have support, facilities and equipment? – What else will be going on at the time?	
What?	– What are the aims and objectives of my presentation? – What should the content of the talk be?	

Note. You might like to take a photocopy of Table 2.5 to use when planning your talk. You could also include it in your report.

TABLE 2.5 *Factors to consider when planning a talk*

If, for example, you are making your presentation to staff in a care setting such as a residential unit, it would be wise to make sure that your event does not clash with something else that is taking place at the time (such as serving tea or other group sessions like dancing). Although your talk will only last 5–10 minutes, you will need to allow extra time for setting up, people arriving and settling down, the general conversation that usually goes on after a presentation (and you may wish to collect feedback from your audience immediately after you have finished), and then clearing away. This means you will need to schedule about an hour for the whole process.

A detailed checklist concerning the setting and timing of the event is given at the end of this section.

Natalie has to schedule her talk for a time when there will be no other lectures or teaching sessions, so that her fellow students are free to attend. She also needs to make sure that her tutor can be present. After checking it out, she decides that a Thursday afternoon would be the best time to make her presentation.

Where will the talk take place?

It is vital to find out where your talk will take place as early as you can. You will need to know whether it will be in a room that is normally used for something else (in which case, you will have to allow plenty of time for setting up, arranging furniture and so on), or whether it is a room dedicated to this kind of activity.

The room must be big enough to accommodate the number of people you are expecting, with adequate heating and ventilation. There must be enough chairs for everyone, and you may choose to include tables if you plan to ask people to write or to do some other kind of activity that requires surfaces to lean on.

It may be important to check out whether or not there will be another activity taking place at the same time that may affect your talk. For example, if you will be presenting in a day unit, and there is a music class taking place at the same time, you need to be sure that the noise from this group will not disturb your talk.

Natalie is lucky. Her college is making available a seminar room for the event to take place. The seminar room is fully equipped with flipchart, whiteboard and OHP, although Natalie may use Powerpoint for her support materials. The room is soundproof, so there will be no danger of disturbance from outside. Good heating, lighting and ventilation are a feature of this room. The talk is taking place in January, but Natalie doesn't need to worry that her group will be too cold, as the temperature in the seminar room is thermostatically controlled.

What are my aims and objectives?

The setting of clear aims and objectives is critical to the success of a presentation. As the saying has it, if you don't know where you are going, the chances are you will end up somewhere else.

You can think of an aim as the point you want to be at the end of a process, in this case a presentation. Objectives are the small steps you need to take to get there. Some examples of aims and objectives are set out in Table 2.6.

For a short presentation of 5–10 minutes it is likely that there will be only one aim. You will have noticed, by studying Table 2.6, that an aim can be expressed as what you hope to achieve by giving your talk. In the three examples in Table 2.6, the speakers have set out where they want to get to in very broad terms. It will take only ten minutes, after all, so the aims are limited by time. It is important, therefore, that your aims are realistic. The first speaker hopes simply to create an awareness of the kinds of problems faced by Deaf students. The second focuses specifically on one kind of activity with service users – the reminiscence session (in which intellectual activity is stimulated by the use of objects to trigger memory). The third (which is Natalie's presentation) looks at one aspect of working with people with learning disabilities – that of empowering them to make their views known.

Objectives deal with the steps needed to achieve the aim. They can be expressed in terms of what the audience will be able to do as a result of the information contained in your talk. Because the presentation is so short, these will often be limited to cognitive outcomes like 'knowing' or 'recognising' something. However, if you choose

AIM (WHAT YOU PLAN TO ACHIEVE WITH YOUR TALK)	OBJECTIVES (WHAT THE AUDIENCE WILL BE ABLE TO DO AT THE END OF THE TALK)
Create an awareness of the problems encountered by Deaf students.	Recognise specific issues for Deaf students with particular reference to: * missing key points in class * misunderstanding what people are saying (social issue) * being excluded from social and study activities
Explain how reminiscence sessions can be used to build relationships between staff and service users in a day unit for older people.	Know how communication can be stimulated by the use of: * old photographs and objects to trigger memories * active listening by staff * skilled facilitation
Explain some methods that can be used to ensure that people with learning disabilities can express their views and wishes.	Know how facilitation can be used to help people with learning disabilities express their views. Recognise other techniques including: * advocacy * self-advocacy * self-directed support

TABLE 2.6 *Aims and objectives of a presentation*

to talk about something practical like using a couple of BSL signs, the objectives might refer to practical outcomes like 'using the signs for . . .'. Specific objectives will make for a successful presentation.

In Natalie's case, she wants to focus specifically on how facilitated sessions can be used to find out the views and preferences of people with learning disabilities. She really only has time in the ten minutes allowed to explain this technique fully. However, she has researched other techniques such as advocacy and self-directed support, so she wants to explain these briefly, and decides to give her audience some additional material about these in a handout. She also hopes that the group will ask her questions, giving her the chance to give them some further information.

The analysis that Natalie did in answering the questions 'Who?', 'When?' and 'Where?' has

helped her to focus on her aims and objectives. She feels that her fellow students will be interested to hear about the facilitated session she took part in at the day unit, and some more theoretical material about a range of communication techniques. She hopes that the relatively small group size will encourage questions, and she feels that the group will appreciate having a handout to support the presented material.

Natalie still has to arrange the information she has collected into the order in which she will present it. There is more advice on how to do this in the next section.

Delivering the talk

When delivering a presentation a speaker has to manage three things: the material (i.e. the content of the talk), the audience and him or herself.

FIGURE 2.19 *Managing Your Material*

There is a saying about giving a good talk. First of all you tell the audience what you are going to tell them (the introduction); then you tell them (the main body of your talk); then you tell them what you've just told them (the summary and conclusion at the end).

The structure of a talk

TELL THEM what you are going to tell them

TELL THEM

TELL THEM what you've just told them

This is a tried-and-tested approach used by public speakers, whether they are politicians, salespeople or entertainers. Good teachers and lecturers also use this structure. The important aspect of this system is that it uses the principle of repetition, which is also a central aspect of teaching and learning.

If you set out what your talk will be about in a clear and memorable introduction, you have created an expectation in your audience about what they will hear. The central body of your talk should then elaborate on these points, using only information or material that is relevant. A summary and conclusion will remind the audience about what they have just heard, and make it more likely that they will remember the key aspects of the talk. People who are taking notes at a talk always appreciate a speaker who keeps to the point, and follows a structure as laid out in the introduction.

The key points of a talk will be designed to achieve the aims and objectives that have already

been decided. This is critical. There is no point is telling your audience to expect a talk on communicating with children, and then digressing to include a mass of anecdotes about working with older people.

The same is true of any supplementary material that you decide to use. Visual material should enhance the points you are making. This might be carefully chosen photographs, or projected images showing the points you are making in bullet-point form. It is a mistake to show too much printed or written material on an overhead – it will be too much for your audience to take in, and can detract from what you are actually saying.

If you are using audio-visual aids such as a video, DVD or CD recording, make sure that you know how to use the equipment that will be available to you on the day. For a short talk, it is advisable to keep the use of such supplementary material to a minimum.

If there is too much material for 10 minutes, but you feel it is really vital to tell the audience about certain things, handouts can be used to give out additional information. Handouts can also be used to reinforce the key points of the talk.

Although you will have to write out the text of your presentation in full to put in the report, you might like to consider using a more abbreviated form for the actual presentation. Some people use prompt cards, on which are written the main points. They then speak naturally when elaborating on these key items. Other people write out the key points onto a sheet of paper.

Whatever method you use on the day, it's a good idea to have a rehearsal beforehand, and to time yourself. You may be surprised at how short 10 minutes is, and find that you have too much material for the time allowed. Record how much time you spend on each topic, and decide whether or not you have the balance right. Make sure you allocate more time to the most important items, but also make sure you don't run out of time completely.

Natalie has decided to introduce her topic with a short account of the facilitated session she attended at the day unit. This will allow her to tell her audience what the talk is to be about. She

MANAGING YOUR MATERIAL	
Structure your talk	Introduction Body of talk Summary/conclusion
Link your talk to your aims and objectives	Choose relevant material that supports your case
Audiovisual material	Keep to a minimum for a short talk Make sure you can use the equipment
Aides memoires	Options include: Reading from full text Prompt cards Notes on sheets of paper
Visual aids	Should be clear and concise Use white space to effect (do not clutter your overheads with too many words) Should enhance (not detract from) your talk
Supplementary material	You can use handouts to give extra material
Rehearse your talk	Always have at least one run-through before the actual event Make sure you keep to time Allocate time to each item

TABLE 2.7 *Tips for managing your material*

then makes several key points about the technique of facilitation. She gives these in bullet-point form on an overhead to complement what she is saying. She then briefly explains that there are a number of other techniques that can be used to help people with learning disabilities to express their views, listing them in the form of bullet-points on an overhead. She tells her audience that she does not have time to describe these fully, but that she is giving them a handout with additional information, including how they can find out more if they are interested.

Managing the audience

Giving a talk is not just a simple matter of standing in front of a group of people and speaking to them. An audience has to be managed in order to create the right environment for listening and learning.

It is important to establish a rapport with a group by exhibiting a friendly and open demeanour. Eye contact can play an important part in this, but it is necessary to maintain a balance between avoiding eye contact completely and making people feel intimidated by staring at them. Remember, too, that some cultural groups may find too much eye contact insulting. Some people (for example, some Muslims) may avoid making eye contact with a speaker.

The physical conditions in the room are also an important consideration. People's concentration will be affected if a room is too hot or cold, too stuffy or too crowded. It is really important for an audience to be comfortable and therefore able to concentrate well if the message is to be delivered effectively.

Creating the right furniture arrangement is also essential in ensuring that your audience is comfortable. Assuming that the chairs are not

A semi-circular arrangement can enhance communication with a small group

fixed, you might want to consider whether the group should sit in a semi-circle or in rows. Larger groups are easier to manage in rows, but the semi-circular arrangement can help to enhance communication between speaker and audience when the group is small.

It is important to make sure that the room is safe. For example, there should be no trailing cables for people to fall over, and the room should not be overcrowded with furniture.

Finally, but no less important, you should take into account the potential needs of people with disabilities, or people for whom English is not a first language. A Deaf person, for example, may need to have a Signer present, and you will certainly need to think about where you position yourself in relation to someone who has a hearing problem. If the audience is to include a Blind person, you should consider having your material prepared in Braille, or make someone available to read the content of the handouts or to take notes. Someone with a physical disability may need more space (for example, if he or she uses a wheelchair). A person with a learning disability may wish to bring along a helper or advocate to make sure that he or she is fully included in the event. Someone for whom English is not a first language may need an interpreter to help explain the key points of the talk.

Natalie's group includes a Deaf student, so she allows space for this person's signer to join. She has opted for a semi-circular chair arrangement, and places a table centre-front on which she can put her laptop, her notes and the handouts. The signer will stand next to Natalie and opposite the Deaf student, who will sit in the centre of the semi-circle. The seminar room has good lighting, heating and ventilation, but she goes along well in advance of the start of the talk to set the thermostat at an appropriate setting for the temperature that day. All cables are properly covered by ducting in this room. However, it is a good idea to take along some masking tape if you are working in a room where equipment is not fitted – any loose cables can then be taped to the floor for the duration of the session.

MANAGING THE AUDIENCE	
Creating a rapport	A friendly attitude is helpful. Eye contact should be appropriate.
Physical comfort	Make sure the room temperature is comfortable. Ventilation should be adequate. Lighting should be adequate.
Furniture	Consider how best to arrange furniture: rows, semi-circle, small groups around tables.
Health & safety	Safety is paramount: ensure no trailing cables, no overcrowding.
Special requirements	Plan for people with sensory, physical or learning disabilities, and people for whom English is not a first language.

TABLE 2.8 *Tips for managing the audience*

Managing yourself

You will be the centre of attention during your talk, so how you manage your voice and body language will be critical.

It is important to speak at a speed that is neither too fast (which will leave people wondering what you have said) nor too slow (which may be boring and result in inattentiveness). Pacing out your talk, not being afraid of making short pauses to allow people to assimilate your words, is also helpful. A silence of about two or three seconds may seem like a long time to you, but in fact it does not seem very long to those who are listening and can be of tremendous help when people are concentrating on what you are saying.

Your voice should be loud enough to be heard by people sitting at the back of the group, although if there is amplification it will be important to speak at a more normal level. Try to vary the pitch of your voice, giving emphasis to the words or phrases that you consider to be more important than others.

Taking a few deep breaths before you start will improve your performance, as will keeping your head up, your spine straight and your shoulders back. Slouching will give a negative impression, and will also prevent you from breathing properly.

Choose your words carefully, and adapt your style of speaking to suit the needs of the audience. A group of non-specialists, for example, may not appreciate being bombarded with a lot of jargon or acronyms that they are unfamiliar with. It is always a good idea to explain any abbreviations or acronyms that you use, just in case there is someone in the audience who is unfamiliar with these terms; specialist terminology (such as Person Centred Planning, or Valuing People) also needs to be explained.

Just as when writing a report or essay, it is a good idea to open each topic or item with a straightforward sentence or statement about what you are going to talk about. For example, 'I am now going to describe three methods that can be used to communicate with people who have a hearing impairment.' It can be a good idea to alternate longer and shorter sentences.

Consider where you will stand in relation to your audience, and whether or not you will need to move about at all. Carefully paced movement (perhaps from one side to the OHP to change an overhead, and than back to your original place) can sometimes enhance a presentation by giving the audience the chance to alter their focus. However, in a very short presentation such as this one, such a tactic would only be of use perhaps once. Too much movement can be distracting.

Similarly, you should avoid unnecessary distracting mannerisms such as head-scratching or hand-waving. These can get in the way of the audience's concentration.

You may choose to sit to give your presentation. This would be appropriate for an intimate group where one of your aims is to engage in a significant amount of interaction. On the other hand, perhaps you have a particular condition which prevents you from standing for any length of time. If sitting down is your choice, for whatever reason, it is important to consider how you can maximise your impact as a speaker – perhaps by ensuring that you are a little higher than the audience, or allowing a little more space between yourself and them so that everyone can see you clearly.

Eye contact should be appropriate (see above), as should your facial expression. You should aim to communicate confidence, interest in the topic and responsiveness to your audience. If you have allowed space for the audience to ask questions, show that you appreciate their response, and treat each questioner with respect, even if you think that the question is irrelevant, or that you have already dealt with that topic.

Sometimes, a speaker will open a talk with a joke or amusing anecdote. This is usually best left to people who are very experienced, as a badly told joke can fall very flat. At worst, it may offend somebody. Only use humour if you are totally sure about your audience's background. You should never tell jokes that stereotype or offend somebody's race, religion or disability.

Finally, using the technique of visualisation in the run-up to the event can help to keep nerves under control. The idea is to imagine yourself in the exact room where you will give your talk, with the audience as far as you know it to be. In your mind's eye, go through the talk, imagining that you are confident and clear, and that your audience is responsive and positive. Sportspeople often use this technique to maximise success in sporting events. It can work just as well for presentations. Creating an expectation of a positive outcome can make the difference between a mediocre performance and an outstanding one.

In the week before she is due to give her talk, Natalie rehearses several times, using the cards she has prepared. She also spends some time each day visualising herself in the seminar room, giving a successful presentation to her fellow-students. On the day, before the event, she has a few quiet minutes during which she does some breathing exercises. She is very excited about the topic, and this enthusiasm helps her to present naturally and clearly. As the group is fairly small, she does not need to raise her voice, and she is helped by the acoustics in the seminar room, which are good. There are some questions, which she is able to deal with very well (she has done her homework).

MANAGING YOURSELF	
Before the event	* Visualise yourself giving a superb presentation * See the audience appreciating your talk, asking interesting questions * See yourself after the talk, discussing it with your tutor
Just before you start	* A few deep breaths will calm the nerves
Voice	* Consider pitch, tone and volume * Speed should be neither too fast nor too slow * Short pauses can assist assimilation of information
Words	* Choose words carefully * Make sentences appropriate to needs of your listeners * Explain any acronyms or abbreviations * Explain any specialist terminology * Explain each topic/item clearly
Position	* Consider whether you will stand or sit * Choose your position carefully * A little movement can assist concentration * Too much movement can be distracting * Mannerisms may annoy
Eyes and face	* Eye contact should be appropriate * Facial expression appropriate * Convey confidence, interest, responsiveness
Humour	* Be careful about using humour * Only use if you are totally sure about your audience

TABLE 2.9 *Tips for managing yourself*

2.7 Feedback research

Collecting feedback

It is essential to get feedback on your performance. This can help you to improve your technique for future occasions. It is also a requirement of this unit that properly documented and researched feedback is obtained.

Structured data

Data of this kind can be **structured** or **unstructured**. Structured data is the kind of information which is uniform – that is, it is collected in the same format from everyone who gives information or feedback. A questionnaire requiring the ticking of boxes, or allocation of a rating to specified parameters provides structured data. Some examples of structured data are given in Table 2.10.

Data can also be structured by asking all respondents the same questions in the same way. Closed questions (i.e. those that can be answered 'yes' or 'no') will give responses that can be directly compared with each other.

Examples of closed questions:

✳ Did you find the presentation helpful?

✳ Did the speaker use his/her voice well?

✳ Did the speaker allocate time appropriately?

Closed questions and structured data are useful if you want to make a **quantitative analysis** of the feedback. Quantitative analysis gives results that can be expressed in terms of numbers or percentages. Table 2.11 gives an example of a quantitative analysis of a presentation from a questionnaire.

To make the presentation clearer, you might choose to set out this table with only the 'Yes' column. However, if some people left boxes

EXAMPLES OF STRUCTURED DATA:		
Tick box questionnaire		Agree Disagree
	Visuals were effective	☐ ☐
	Presentation was clear	☐ ☐
Rating scale questionnaire	Give a rating for each of the following parameters by circling the appropriate score (1 = low; 5 = high)	
	Low Score High Score	
	Visual aids 1 2 3 4 5	
	Presentation 1 2 3 4 5	

TABLE 2.10 *Some examples of structured data*

ANALYSIS OF END-OF-SESSION QUESTIONNAIRE 15 PEOPLE ATTENDED THIS TALK; 12 QUESTIONNAIRES WERE COMPLETED.				
	YES		NO	
	Number	Percentage	Number	Percentage
Was the presentation clear?	11	92%	1	8%
Were the visual materials effective?	11	92%	1	8%
Were the handouts helpful?	7	58%	5	42%
Was the venue pleasant?	7	58%	5	42%

TABLE 2.11 *Example of a quantitative analysis of a presentation*

unticked, you might want to make this clear by adding an additional column for a 'no answer'.

Using this method of data collection and analysis, it is possible to conclude that over 90 per cent of those attending the talk felt that the presentation was clear and the visual materials were effective. There was less satisfaction with the quality of the handouts, and also with the venue.

The rating scale method of structured data collection makes possible a more precise analysis of what the audience really thought of a presentation, as Table 2.12 shows.

This analysis of the audience's response to the same talk is more specific. It shows that while 11 people gave the presentation and visuals a very high score (4–5 on the rating scale), the level of dissatisfaction with handouts and venue was considerable. Ten people (83 per cent) rated the handouts at poor to adequate (scores 1–3), while all 12 gave a similar low rating to the venue. The scores can be aggregated for presentation purposes, as Table 2.13 shows.

Collected rating-scale information has given this speaker clear information to take into account when evaluating the talk. There was something about the handouts that the majority of people did not like, and a review of this material is called for. However, the audience was unanimous in having reservations about the venue, and unless there are very good reasons for this (perhaps the room was too hot or too cold) the speaker would be advised to think very carefully before booking this venue again. He or she should certainly investigate this response further.

Presenting quantitative data

As well as presenting quantitative material in the form of tables, bar charts and pie charts may also be used to give a more graphic representation of audience response. An example of both a bar chart and a pie chart are given in Figure 2.20, using data from Table 2.13.

ANALYSIS OF END-OF-SESSION QUESTIONNAIRE 15 PEOPLE ATTENDED THIS TALK: 12 QUESTIONNAIRES WERE COMPLETED 1 = LOW SCORE: 5 = HIGH SCORE					
Parameter	Rating				
	1	2	3	4	5
Clarity of presentation			1	9	2
Effectiveness of visual aids			1	9	2
Helpfulness of handouts		5	5	2	
Venue		6	6		

TABLE 2.12 *Example of analysis of end-of-session questionnaire using the rating scale method of structured data collection*

ANALYSIS OF END-OF SESSION QUESTIONNAIRES AGGREGATED SCORES		
	Poor–Adequate	Good–Very good
Clarity of presentation	1 (8%)	11 (92%)
Effectiveness of visuals	1 (8%)	11 (92%)
Helpfulness of handouts	10 (83%)	2 (17%)
Venue	12 (100%)	

TABLE 2.13 *Analysis of end-of session questionnaires showing aggregated scores*

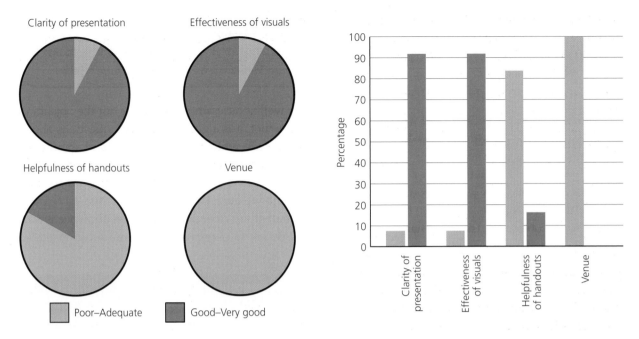

Clarity of presentation | Effectiveness of visuals

Helpfulness of handouts | Venue

Poor–Adequate | Good–Very good

FIGURE 2.20 *Graphic representation of audience response*

Unstructured data

Many questionnaires contain areas for respondents to add their own comments on whatever topics they wish, and in their own words. This kind of information is known as unstructured data. Such information is harder to quantify than structured data, and is sometimes referred to as **qualitative data**. Qualitative data is also often collected by interview. (Quantitative data can also be collected in this way. If so, the researcher ticks the boxes for the respondent.) Open questions are often used to collect this kind of information. Open questions are those that cannot be answered 'Yes' or 'No'. They often begin with the words 'What' and 'Why'.

Examples of open questions are:

∗ What are your views about the talk you have just heard?

∗ What did you think about the venue?

∗ Why did you choose to attend this talk?

Sometimes, this kind of data is referred to as semi-structured, because it invites responses about a specific topic, while leaving respondents free to answer in their own words.

Examples of questions to collect semi-structured data:

∗ Were there any topics not covered in the talk that you would like to have had included?

∗ What did you think of the time allocation for each topic?

∗ How could this talk have been improved?

Totally unstructured data is collected by leaving a space on the questionnaire for audience members to express their own views in their own way on whatever issues they want. This may give some valuable information that was not anticipated. In the case of the hypothetical talk analysed in the tables above, some of the audience may have used free space to explain why they gave the venue such a low score. Perhaps the chairs were uncomfortable in the room, or maybe the facilities in the venue were less than adequate.

A good questionnaire will usually gather a mixture of quantitative and qualitative data. The quantitative data set will allow for some precision in measuring audience satisfaction, while space for the freer qualitative material may raise valuable points that would otherwise not have been mentioned.

2.8 Evaluating communication skills

Evaluating your performance

An essential aspect of professional work is reflection and self-assessment, in order to evaluate what has been achieved.

A good way of evaluating your performance is to check it against the objectives you set at the start of the planning process. If you have achieved the objectives, then the chances are you gave a good talk.

> **Key concept**
>
> *Evaluation:* to evaluate something is to assess it, in particular its worth, value or importance.

As well as assessing whether or not the objectives were met, it is a good idea to ask questions about the way in which you performed, and about other aspects of the total event. The planning checklists in this unit might be used as the basis for a self-evaluative exercise, as the questionnaire demonstrates. Feedback from the audience is vital if you are to improve your communication skills.

EVALUATING YOUR PERFORMANCE USE THIS QUESTIONNAIRE TO EVALUATE YOUR PERFORMANCE AFTER GIVING YOUR TALK. GIVE YOURSELF A RATING FROM 1–5 FOR EACH OF THE FOLLOWING PARAMETERS (1 = LOW SCORE, 5 = HIGHEST SCORE).	
MANAGING THE MATERIAL	**Score (1–5)**
Introduction to the talk	
Main body of talk	
Summary/conclusion	
Meeting aims/objectives	
Visual aids	
Audiovisual material	
Supplementary material	
Use of notes/written text, etc.	
MANAGING THE AUDIENCE	
Creating a rapport	
Physical comfort of audience	
Furniture arrangement	
Health & safety Issues	
Use of equipment	
Attention to special requirements (e.g. use of signer, etc.)	
MANAGING YOURSELF	
Use of voice (pitch, tone, volume)	
Speed of delivery	
Choice of words	
Use of humour (if applicable)	
Use of body: position, mannerisms, etc.	
Eye contact/facial expression	
On reflection, would you do anything differently next time?	
Use this space to record anything else about your performance that you feel is relevant.	

TABLE 2.14 *Example of a questionnaire*

PLANNING TO GIVE A TALK: SOME PRACTICAL CONSIDERATIONS		NOTES
Is your talk one of a series of presentations planned for the same day?	If 'yes', you will need to be very clear about how your talk fits in, both in terms of timing and content.	
What time of day would be best for the talk?	Is your audience likely to be tired, or to be distracted by something that is happening afterwards?	
What else may be going on at the same time?	If you are giving your talk in a social services unit, for example, make sure that your activity does not clash with other important daily events, or that another activity does not impinge on what you are doing (e.g. a noisy activity in the room next door).	
Is the room the right size for the expected audience?	How big will the audience be?	
What furniture and/or equipment will you need?	Tables? Straight-backed chairs? TV/video/DVD player? etc.	
What facilities will you need?	Powerpoint? Loop system? Strong lighting? etc.	
Is there easy access to the room/building?	Do you need a ramp/lift? Handrails? Wide doors for access by people in wheelchairs? etc.	
What additional help will you need?	Signer/communicator for people who are Deaf/hearing impaired? Personal helper for someone with a mobility problem? Communicator/translator for someone who does not use English as a first language?	
What other aids or equipment will you need?	Braille translation of written materials? etc.	
What health & safety issues do you need to consider?	Condition of all furniture and equipment (including electrical equipment); Safe access and exit (all emergency exits to be easily accessible) Trip hazards to be eliminated Adequate heating and ventilation, etc. Note. There will be guidance on health & safety in the setting where you give your talk. Be sure to check this out with the manager responsible.	

TABLE 2.15 *Planning to give a talk: a checklist*

The questionnaire in Table 2.14 uses a mix of structured, semi-structured and unstructured data collection. You might consider asking your tutor to use the same questionnaire to record his or her views on your performance.

As with collection of audience feedback, quantitative and qualitative information can be combined to give a balanced evaluation of your performance.

Natalie has saved all the checklists she used during the planning process for her talk. She has designed a feedback questionnaire that uses a mix of structured, semi-structured and unstructured data collection, and has used the format suggested in this unit to self-assess (Checklist Table 2.15, page 95). Her final report uses a mix of quantitative and qualitative data to give a balanced analysis of her performance. She is able to identify a number of areas where she could have done better, but on the whole both she and her tutor are pleased with her performance. It has demonstrated her knowledge of relevant communication skills and issues, together with her ability to self-assess and to collect and analyse data from a variety of sources.

UNIT 2 ASSESSMENT

In the report you produce for this unit, you will need to demonstrate a knowledge of communication skills (together with barriers to communication) in two areas. The first relates to the service user and the setting that you have chosen to study. The second relates to the act of giving a talk.

With respect to the former (i.e. work with a service user), you must demonstrate a theoretical knowledge of communication issues, in terms of the content of your talk and the material you use. With respect to the latter (giving a talk), the actual act of presentation itself constitutes a practical demonstration of your communication skills in this domain. The feedback that you collect from your audience and your tutor will contribute to your evidence about your communication skills. Planning documentation, together with research materials, will also enhance your evidence.

AO1 Knowledge of communication skills; knowledge of chosen topic

You will need to show that you have understood the issues explored in this unit, together with issues that are important for the particular service user you have chosen to describe.

Good marks will be obtained by demonstrating knowledge of:

❋ a range of verbal skills (e.g. using appropriate words and language, etc.)

❋ non-verbal skills (e.g. adapting the voice, observing body language, using eye contact appropriately, respecting personal space, etc.)

❋ barriers to communication (e.g. with people who have a sensory impairment or a learning disability, with people who have a different first language to yourself, conditions such as aphasia, etc.)

Higher marks will be obtained by demonstrating the above plus:

❋ an explanation of techniques and strategies that may be used to overcome barriers to communication (e.g. use of facilitator, use of communicator or signer, etc.)

❋ a clear explanation of the communication issues that are important to the service user in the chosen setting.

❋ use of specialist terminology or key concepts (e.g. para-language, speech community, cultural assumptions, prejudice, etc.).

AO2 Application of communication skills

In giving your talk, good marks will be obtained by:

* confident management of the material, the audience, yourself
* using a range of types of question to collect feedback that includes both quantitative and qualitative data.

Higher marks will be obtained by demonstrating the above, plus:

* evidence of thorough planning for the event
* a thorough exploration of the communication issues that are the subject of the talk.

AO3 Research and analysis

Good marks will be obtained for:

* use of relevant material gathered from a range of sources (including the Internet, printed sources and relevant experts)
* a clear analysis of feedback collected from the audience and your tutor
* a thorough written account that sets out all relevant information, using clear headings to guide the reader.

Higher marks will be obtained by the above, plus:

* a confident and appropriate use of both quantitative and qualitative data collection techniques
* use of specialist vocabulary to interpret information
* use of a comprehensive range of source material to research the talk
* use of a range of expressive devices to present your material, such as tables, bar charts, pie diagrams
* an excellent written account that gives a clear, well-reasoned analysis, combining visual presentation of data with the written text in a complementary way.

Evaluation

After the talk, you will need to reflect on the experience, and then collate your personal thoughts and reactions with the feedback collected from the audience and your tutor.

Good marks will be obtained by:

* a balanced and sound judgement of the effectiveness of the talk and of your own communication skills
* an appraisal of the decisions you made concerning the choice of material and the order in which you presented it
* some suggestions for improving the design of the talk and/or its content
* a clear written account of this analysis, that uses headings to guide the reader.

Higher marks will be obtained by the above, plus:

* effective use of audience feedback in making an evaluation of the talk
* achieving a balance between accepting criticism that is justified, and an assertion of what you did well
* explaining which of your planning decisions you consider (on reflection) to be sound, whilst identifying things that you would do differently
* an excellent written account in which written text and visual presentation of material are complementary.

References

Bales, R. (1970) *Personality and Interpersonal Behaviour,* Holt, Rinehart & Winston, New York

Bostrom, R. N. (1997) 'The process of listening' in Hargie, O.D.W. (Ed.) *The Handbook of Communication Skills* 2nd *Ed.* Routledge, London and New York

Department of Health (2001) *Valuing People: a new strategy for learning disabilitiy for the 21st century. Planning with people: Guidance for Implementation Groups.* Department of Health, London. Can also be accessed via www.valuingpeople.gov.uk

Descombes, C. (2004) *The smoke and mirrors of empowerment: a critique of user-professional partnership* in *Communication, Relationships and Care* Robb, M., Barrett, S., Komaromy, C., and Rogers, A. (Eds) OU & Routledge, London & New York

Engebretson, J. (2004) *Caring Presence: a Case Study* in *Communication, Relationships and Care* Robb, M., Barrett, S., Komaromy, C., and Rogers, A. (Eds) OU & Routledge, London & New York

Hayman, M. (1998) *A Protocol for People with Hearing Impairment* Nursing Times, 28 October, Volume 94, No 43

Rogers, C. R. (1951) *Client Centred Therapy,* Houghton Mifflin, Boston

Tuckman, B. (1965) 'Development Sequence in Small Groups', in *Psychological Bulletin*, Vol 63, No 6

Thompson, T. L. (1986) *Communication for Health Professionals* Harper & Row, New York

Useful websites

Please see www.heinemann.co.uk/hotlinks (express code 1562P) for links to the following websites which may provide a source of information:

* The Valuing People website set up by the government is an excellent source for articles/research about work for and with people with learning disabilities.

* The People First website is a good place to find out about what people with learning disabilities, their advocates and their carers, are saying.

* The In Control organisation promotes communication with people with learning disabilities, especially ways to empower them to express their views and to be involved in Person Centred Planning.

* The British Deaf Association website contains details of BSL.

* The British Sign website includes details of signs and finger spelling alphabet.

* Website of the Royal Association for Deaf People.

* Information on Makaton can be found on their website.

* Further details on Braille are on the Braille Plus website.

UNIT 3

Health, illness and disease

You will learn about:

3.1 Concepts of health and ill health

3.2 Factors affecting health and well-being

3.3 Immunisation against disease

3.4 The value of screening

Introduction

This unit begins by exploring the attitudes and understanding of the concepts of both health and ill health and how individuals and groups of people may view 'health' differently. In developing this theme, an investigation is made into the importance of a selection of major factors affecting health and well-being and the interrelationships between them. Finally, an examination is made of major preventative measures currently being taken to promote health and avoid illness.

How you will be assessed

This unit will be internally assessed. You will need to produce a portfolio containing a questionnaire and two reports.

3.1 Concepts of health and ill health

Defining 'health' is a difficult task to do, as it means different things to different people, rather like 'stress' or 'happiness' does. These socially abstract words are almost indefinable except in the utmost general terms. We must, however, have some idea of the meaning of 'health', as we use the word in all sorts of titles such as health visitor, health care worker, healthy living, health foods, health education and health promotion. Where the word health prefixes an occupational title, it is particularly desirable to understand the meaning of the word in order to establish the nature of the job role.

At this stage, you might like to think about how *you* might define health, bearing in mind the difficulties with care terminology already referred to.

> ### Think it over...
>
> How would you explain your health?

The World Health Organisation, part of the United Nations organisation, was set up in 1948 and at that time defined 'health' as being *'a state of complete physical, mental and social well-being and not merely the absence of disease or infirmity'*. Later on, criticisms about the idealistic nature of 'complete state of well-being' and the unreal, implied view that health is static throughout one's lifespan led to an expansion of this definition by several groups and individuals in the mid-eighties. In effect, this means that there is no single definition of health that everyone uses, so in this unit we will consider three of the most common concepts currently in use. These are:

* a holistic concept of health
* a positive concept of health
* a negative concept of health.

Concepts of health

Holistic

A favoured concept of health might produce a more wholesome or 'holistic' view of health as being in the peak of physical, intellectual, social and emotional fitness. Holism means giving attention to the whole, in this case the whole person. The term must also encompass the environment or surroundings of the individual and take on board social and psychological factors.

Health can be affected by all that is around us, and the individuals whom we have contact with. Although our basic health needs do not change as we progress through the life stages, our surroundings and contacts change all the time, suggesting that in holistic terms, our health changes too. Most care professionals will agree that addressing physical health only is not enough and that we must appreciate the emotional, social, spiritual and intellectual health as well – in fact, the whole person. This concept provides some practical difficulties, as it means that there is no limit to the boundaries of responsibility of health professionals, and consequently the focus of care becomes blurred. Once the focus is regained, there is a risk of

FIGURE 3.1 *The concept of holisitic health*

becoming limited to treating a particular condition or part of the body again – this is often called reductionism.

The broader, holistic focus has been absorbed for some professionals into the term well-being.

Positive

There is also a positive concept of health, which can be equated to the achievement of physical fitness and mental stability. When considering the negative concept below, and discussing that the absence of disease and illness represents health, then that in itself assumes a background of 'normal' health represented by efficient, fully operational physiological and mental function.

The positive concept goes a little way to describing what health is, rather than what it is not.

Seedhouse (1986) proposed health *as a foundation for achieving a person's realistic potential'*. The WHO later offered a revised concept of health as *'the extent to which an individual or group is able, on the one hand, to realise aspirations and satisfy needs, and on the other hand, to change or cope with the environment'*.

Health is now seen as a positive concept that focuses on personal and physical capacities together with social resources, adaptability and responsibility.

Negative

If you ask friends or members of your family what they understand by 'health' or 'being healthy', you will collect varied responses.

Most people will respond in terms of 'not being ill', indicating a rather negative view that health is something that you do not think about until you have not got it. In other words, health is something that you have until your daily life is disturbed by illness and you are unable to carry out your normal programme. When it is difficult to explain a term using clear and definite attributes, people often resort to describing what it is not – a somewhat negative viewpoint. Some individuals might describe happiness as not being sad or regretful, but many people might describe themselves as neither sad nor happy – so there is

a middle position. Similarly, being poor might be thought of as not being rich, but once again many individuals would say they were neither wealthy nor poor, but possess enough money to supply their basic needs. Clearly then, negative descriptions, while they might be helpful, do not provide a full picture and are simple to use in the absence of positive characteristics.

Terms such as these are also relative to their context; a wealthy businessman who has lost several hundred thousand pounds in a bad business venture, might describe himself as poor, even though he has several functioning businesses and a large bank account. An elderly senior citizen, having just won £20 on a lottery ticket might describe herself as rich. The context of such words can therefore be extremely important in their interpretation. Health and well-being can thus be considered as a negative concept when described as the absence of physical illness, disease and/or mental disorder. This concept has fallen out of favour in current care concepts, but it is a description that the general public still frequently employs.

Other terminology in current use

Well-being

Well-being is just as difficult to explain as health! Even theorists cannot agree on the meaning although many feel that it is partly subjective, what we wish it to be for ourselves, and partly objective because it must have something to do with 'wellness' and some people do not make healthy lifestyle choices. Dictionary definitions do not help either; some equate well-being with welfare, a person's satisfactory condition, and others with flourishing and thriving.

Personal notions of health

Some people might provide you with a very personal notion of health, such as 'when my rheumatism isn't giving me trouble'. Personal views like this might depend on age, social background, culture, circumstances and experience as seen in the mini-case studies below.

SCENARIO

* Simon probably links the perception of his health to his basketball prowess and considers himself 'ill' if he cannot attend to practise due to physical ailments.

* Maria associates health with decent accommodation and being with her family; she is unlikely to worry about minor problems of physical health, like colds.

* Stan is likely to concentrate on meeting his friends; he is likely to dismiss his bronchitis and arthritis as being natural because of his age and previous occupation. When he cannot manage his little outing then life is more of a burden.

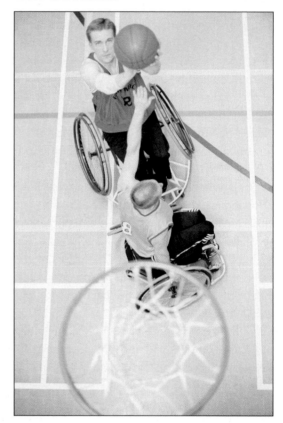

Disability does not prevent people from being active

The scenarios show how each person's view of 'health' is different and closely linked to feelings, moods and being able to cope with daily activities, jobs or events.

Other people, especially those with different cultural inheritances, may view health as a spiritual form of well-being; for example, in Islam, consuming alcohol is seen as an unholy thing to do, as it leads to loss of self-control.

Many Christians believe that they can only be truly healthy when they have accepted the teachings of Christ and not whether they feel ill or not. Vegans and vegetarians often believe that eating meat is not healthy. Other religious and non-religious groups have different views of health.

Holistic health means considering the whole person and not just the illness or disorder, whereas positive health stresses achieving potential and satisfying needs and hopes as well as having efficient, working organ systems and physiological 'wholeness'. Some groups still use negative concepts to describe their health in terms of absence of disease or infirmity.

Concept of ill health

Terms signifying ill health are in general parlance interchangeable, but in health terminology, they have more specific meanings. Illness tends to be a word that we use ourselves (i.e. a subjective sensation) to describe a situation that exists if we feel less than well, either physically or mentally.

For example, we may say 'I have to leave because I am feeling ill'. Rarely, do we say, 'I have to go home because I have a disease', probably because we feel unqualified to make that statement. This example illustrates the difference between illness and disease, although we have a tendency to interchange them in prose. Illness, then is something that we feel, a sense of 'unwell-ness' that is personal to us at certain times. Disease is more specific, an 'unwell-ness' that has some pathological basis; it can be diagnosed and named, has certain signs and symptoms, possible treatment and an outcome.

We can feel ill without having a disease and have a disease without feeling ill; we can also feel ill with a disease.

Another term, more easily defined, is disorder that, as the name suggests, is a malfunctioning of part of the body but once again is often used as a replacement for illness and disease.

Summary

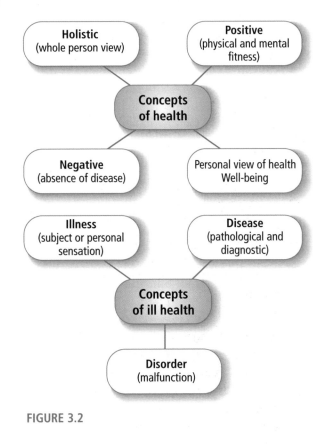

FIGURE 3.2

Three old friends are meeting for a meal, which they try to do once a month; last month, they all cancelled due to health problems and they spend time telling each other about their illnesses.

* Joe said that he was feeling 'under the weather' and was unable to carry out his usual activities, but got better after a few days.

* Brian said that he had gastro-enteritis from a chill-cook ready meal that he had kept for too long in the refrigerator before eating.

* Sam told them that his knee was 'playing up'.

Using concepts – can you?
1 Decide on a suitable term to use for the three problems of ill health.

2 Explain the reasons for your choices.

Using concepts, can you analyse issues?
3 Discuss the problems encountered in defining the term 'health'.

Using concepts, can you evaluate issues?
4 Holistic health can be viewed as the most desirable definition of health. Explain the values of holistic health.

3.2 Factors affecting health and well-being

Not everyone is fortunate to be healthy and many factors affect an individual's quality of health. Some factors may be outside a person's control, such as poverty and inherited diseases, and thus lead to a low health experience. For a large number of people, however, good health is dependent on lifestyle choices and habits; yet still individuals gamble with their health. Many healthy people are fully aware of the risks they take but feel that poor health is an experience that others suffer from and not themselves.

There are many factors that affect health and well-being and many are inter-related in an important ways. Some factors to be considered are shown in Figure 3.3.

Eating sensibly in order to maintain a balanced diet

A balanced diet is an important part of a healthy lifestyle. Food is a basic human need, as it drives the body processes; we can think of food as fuel rather like the petrol or diesel that drives a motor car. A lack of food fuel, or the wrong type, can result in poor physiological performance and, consequently, less effective work and play and the likelihood of illness and even death.

Food contains nutrients (substances that nourish) that allow the body to grow, develop and function in the correct way. Some components of food, chiefly fats and carbohydrates, provide energy to carry out physiological work, while proteins are necessary to form the structures of the body such as cells, many hormones and vital enzymes. These three named components all contribute to our calorie (or in SI units, joule) intake and should form the bulk of a diet.

Vitamins and minerals, on the other hand, do not contribute to energy requirements, but are, nevertheless, just as essential to the normal functioning of the human body, although they are only required in small quantities. Water constitutes a major part of the human body and is essential to life processes. An individual who is deprived of both water and food would die from lack of water first. Fibre, or roughage, is also an important part of a diet, as it assists in moving food along the digestive tract, prevents many bowel disorders and adds bulk to food without providing calories.

Table 3.1 provides a list of some of the major foods supplying dietary requirements.

A balanced diet is one that provides carbohydrates, fats and proteins in the correct proportions and adequate vitamins, mineral elements, fibre and water for healthy living.

Planning a balanced diet can be a complex process in terms of energy requirements, size of portions and so on; most people, however, manage diets without recourse to lengthy volumes of food energy tables. Approximately 60

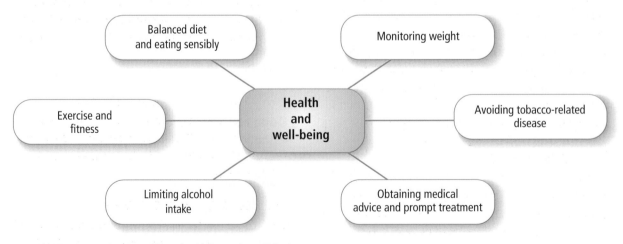

FIGURE 3.3 *Factors that affect health and well-being*

FOOD COMPONENT	COMMON FOODS SUPPLYING BASIC NEEDS FOR THE COMPONENT
Carbohydrate	Bread, pasta, rice, potatoes, cakes, biscuits, cereals
Fats	Butter, lard, suet, oils, margarine
Protein	Meat, milk, fish, eggs, milk, soy beans, legumes
Vitamins	Fresh fruit, fresh vegetables, dairy products
Mineral elements	Fresh fruit and vegetables
Fibre (roughage)	Cereals, fresh fruit and vegetables
Water	Water in drinks, most foods

TABLE 3.1 *Some major foods supplying dietary requirements*

per cent of meals should be in the form of carbohydrates, 20 per cent as fats and 20 per cent as proteins. Meals should also contain substantial proportions of fruit and vegetables to fulfil the vitamin, mineral and fibre requirements in individuals diets.

One of the major problems of nutrition in the twenty-first century is the relatively large quantity of hidden fat, sugar and salt found in convenience foods. The pace of life is so much faster than it used to be; many people live very busy lives, which leave little time for food preparation. There is little wonder that convenience foods have become a way of life.

The UK government is so concerned about the growing epidemic of obesity, particularly among school children that there are now a vast number of organisations and committees trying to resolve the issues. One change in the pipeline is the more accurate labelling of food, so that the hidden components are more obvious. Whether busy parents can afford the time to read labels on groceries and have the inclination to act upon that information, however, remains to be seen.

So-called 'healthy' food alternatives are often more expensive and the term in itself can be misleading.

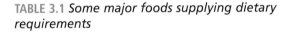

✳ DID YOU KNOW?

Half a can of well-known baked beans contains 10.4 g of sugar (although total carbohydrate content is actually 27.1 g), so a boldly advertised can of low-sugar baked beans may still contain 9.4 g of sugar. Customers who purchase the low-sugar alternative can pay more and feel worthy, although they have in fact only saved 1 g of sugar.

Cans of tuna and sardines in oil or tomato sauce can be bought quite inexpensively, especially in multi-packs, but single tins, in water, are twice as expensive to buy. Manufacturers claim that they have to make them specially and there is not much demand for them. People have been conditioned to taste high salt and sugar levels in prepared food and consequently feel that other preparations do not taste the same.

Another major problem of highly processed foods is the lack of fibre content, most of which has been removed in the processing. An individual who consumes such food rapidly feels hungry again and looks for more food to eat. Wholegrain foods, fruit and vegetables, in addition to containing lower calories, have a 'feel full' factor to them, so dispel hunger for longer periods and provide protection for longer periods. The government-backed 'Five a day' campaign has highlighted a simple message that consuming five pieces/portions of fruit and vegetables each day is an important aid to health for all levels of society.

NACNE and COMA dietary advice

Other recommendations made by NACNE (National Advisory Committee for Nutrition Education) and COMA (Committee on Medical Aspects of Food Policy) include those that are outlined below.

Reduce overall fat intake

Reduce overall fat intake and when fat is part of the diet make sure that as much as possible is polyunsaturated and not saturated (basically, this means minimising animal fats and using plant lipids instead). Lipids or fats and oils contain twice as many calories as carbohydrates and proteins – they are energy-rich. When consumed in a greater quantity than is needed, fat is stored around the body tissues, causing weight gain. As weight increases, the demand for more food to sustain the extra cells also increases and so, too, does the demand for oxygen, pumped blood, hormones like insulin and more substances taking part in metabolism.

Overweight people have a higher risk of developing diabetes, heart disease, strokes, respiratory difficulties and mobility problems, as the excess load on legs, ankles and feet over a period of years takes its toll. Having developed health problems, they are then more likely to suffer accidental injury and problems with surgical care. Organs function less well as arteries become narrowed due to fatty deposits (atheroma) coating the inner walls.

There may be social and emotional problems associated with being overweight to contend with as well as physical problems.

There has been a great deal of recent publicity in the media about the 'epidemic' of eating disorders, both anorexia nervosa and bulimia, and the failure of doctors to recognise these conditions until a late stage has been reached. Indeed, even when such disorders are recognised, there are no specialist services for referral. This is the other side of the coin, and although a distorted perception of body image is considered to be a psychological condition, it has also been appreciated that psychiatric wards are not appropriate care environments for the young people (mostly teenage girls and young women) who have these disorders. Clearly, this too has to be considered as an example of individuals *not* eating sensibly. Individuals who suffer with these complaints have a morbid fear of being fat, and see themselves as fat even when they are several stones underweight. Induced vomiting is common and regular in both disorders, that of bulimia following bouts of binge eating.

Eat less salt

Salt attracts water and when combined they are thought to contribute to raised blood pressure with consequent, heart and circulation problems, kidney disorders, cerebral strokes and haemorrhages. The human body requires some salt, but there is enough in natural plant materials without the need to add more salt in cooking. We have become conditioned to a high salt intake as a result of eating processed foods. People who suffer from hypertension are advised to refrain from adding salt to cooking or plated meals. Herbs and spices can be used to flavour food instead of salt.

Reduce intake of sugar

Sugar provides calories without providing any other benefits; this is often known as 'empty' calories. Excess sugar is converted into fat for storage, so eating too much sugar leads to the same health problems as too much fat. Consider the effect of consuming only 'junk' food containing surplus energy-rich fat *and* surplus sugar; obesity is just around the corner!

Eat more fibre

The benefits of fibre, fruit and vegetables on food and eating are examined on page 105, but rather like a see-saw, feeling satisfied hunger-wise from eating more fibre will also enable us to eat less fat, salt and sugar.

Drink less alcohol

Just like sugar, alcohol provides 'empty' calories resulting in weight gain. (See also limiting alcohol consumption on page 109).

Limit the consumption of certain other foods

There is also good advice on limiting the consumption of red meat and substituting fish or vegetable protein on at least two days of the week.

> **Think it over...**
>
> You need to be aware of different food patterns within different cultures and that by choice or religion many people are vegan, vegetarian or a variation of these.

Taking regular exercise to maintain physical and mental fitness

The Chief Medical Officer in his report *'Call for Action' (April 2004)* quotes:

'The message in this report is clear. The scientific evidence is compelling. Physical activity not only contributes to well-being, but is also essential for good health. People who are physically active reduce their risk of developing major chronic diseases – such as coronary heart disease, stroke and type2 diabetes – by up to 50 per cent, and the risk of premature death by about 20–30 per cent. The annual costs of physical inactivity in England are estimated at £8.2 billion – including the rising costs of treating chronic diseases such as coronary heart disease and diabetes. This does not include the contribution of inactivity to obesity – an estimated further £2.5 billion cost to the economy each year.

This report must be the wake-up call that changes attitudes to active lifestyles in every household. Being active is no longer simply an option – it is essential if we are to live healthy and fulfilling lives into old age.'

The report suggests that a total of 30 minutes of moderately intense physical activity each day for five or more days per week will improve the general health of adults. Furthermore, this can be made up of shorter bouts of activity, such as walking briskly rather than taking motorised transport or using stairs rather than lifts. For many people, 45 minutes to 1 hour of activity may be necessary to prevent obesity. More intensive exercise will bring even greater benefits

Exercise improves health and strength in children

For children and young people, a total of at least 60 minutes per day is necessary with intense activity at least twice a week (such as jumping, skipping, running, gymnastics) to improve bone health, muscle strength and flexibility.

The adult recommendations are also appropriate for older people to enable them to keep moving and retain mobility. More specific activities to improve strength, coordination and balance are particularly beneficial. Independence is further promoted by avoidance of diseases prevalent in older people such as osteoporosis, circulatory disease and depression.

The Chief Medical Officer further states that *'physical activity needs to be seen as an opportunity – for enjoyment, for improved vitality, for a sense of achievement, for fitness, for optimal weight, and – not least – for health. It needs to be seen as enjoyable, and as fun – not as unnecessary effort. Perceptions need to be changed – too many people think they are already active enough.'*

This report identifies physical inactivity as ranking alongside cigarette smoking and unhealthy diets as agents for chronic disease.

Games help develop balance and coordination

Maintaining an active lifestyle is important in order to avoid weight gain, but the most potent combination is physical activity and a healthy diet. This maximises fat loss, keeps lean tissue and promotes both fitness and health benefits.

Research has also shown that moderately intense exercise is beneficial for depression, anxiety, sleep disorders, the effects of stress and cognitive function in older people. Group recreational sports/activities have social and emotional benefits but activities, best described as rhythmic, such as dancing, jogging, cycling, swimming and brisk walking, are most effective.

Children are in danger of becoming 'couch potatoes'

Protection against some cancers is also enhanced with an active lifestyle; the incidence of colon cancer is 50 per cent less likely in those who are intensely active than in inactive people. There may also be reductions in breast cancer in post-menopausal women and lung cancer amongst those who are physically active.

Physical inactivity is not an option; the encouragement of an active lifestyle is essential in order to reduce the number of chronic conditions and to promote better health.

Many girls and women, particularly from Asian cultures, do not undertake much sport or exercise because of strict dress codes; and other groups, like older people, consider exercise is only necessary for young people.

This section has shown how regular exercise and eating sensibly are interrelated in the way that health is maintained.

Monitoring weight in order to avoid weight-related illness or even premature death

Weight or mass in relation to height and frame size is a routine measurement of physical health. It is also used as an indicator of growth in children. Healthy adults can maintain a fairly stable weight, as input of energy in the form of food and drink should balance the amount of energy loss from physical activity and metabolic activity. When there is an imbalance, there are implications, certainly in the long-term for health and well-being. Here, we can see the interrelationships between eating sensibly, exercising regularly and monitoring weight.

Most people monitor their weight informally on bathroom scales, noticing whether they have gained or lost weight since the last time they weighed themselves. Few people actually act on this knowledge by redressing the balance – either cutting down on food intake, or selected parts of it, or increasing physical activities. People are even less likely to refer to charts or graphs for monitoring purpose (see Figure 3.4). Some might attempt a slimming diet for a few weeks or join a gymnasium, but this is usually short-term.

Commercial interests make huge sums of money from both gymnasium members who never actually use the gym and slimming foods and meals that work in the short-term. Even the

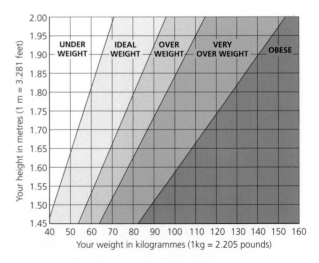

FIGURE 3.4 *Weight and height charts*

media have joined the bandwagon! In January of every year, practically every tabloid newspaper and magazine publishes a 'guaranteed' slimming diet and reality TV features celebrities and non-celebrities trying to lose weight.

The sad fact is that it takes a long time to regain a normal weight for height, often years, because individuals watch their weight increasing by a few pounds each year before they act. Apart from using weighing scales, there are other signs that people ignore such as:

* normal clothing is too loose or too tight

* requiring larger or smaller sizes in clothing

* being uncomfortable in hot or cold weather

* friends remarking on changed appearance

* being disinclined to undertake physical activity.

An individual is considered to be obese if his or her body weight is 20 per cent or more than that given in a standard height/weight chart. Obesity results in significantly increased incidence of:

* high blood pressure

* stroke

* coronary artery disease

* type 2 diabetes (mature onset)

* cancers of the colon, rectum and prostate

* cancers of the breast, cervix and uterus

* aggravation of osteo-arthritis, hip, knee, and back pain

* decreased mobility causing a vicious circle of more weight gain.

Only a very few people are overweight because of gland disorders but many have a genetic predisposition to obesity. Fat people are often part of fat families.

Weight loss may occur as part of a deliberate weight reduction plan, or because food intake has been reduced or activity increased. More serious implications for loss of weight are:

* depression lowers motivation to eat

* ulcer pain may cause food avoidance

* eating disorders such as anorexia nervosa or bulimia

* illness causing severe vomiting

* untreated type 1 diabetes (juvenile onset)

* nearly all cancers

* chronic infection such as tuberculosis

* hormonal problems such as hyperthyroidism.

It is clear from these two lists that it is important to monitor weight to avoid chronic illness and premature death.

People from ethnic groups who wear loose clothes may not be aware of weight changes quite as easily as those who wear Western styles; they are also less likely to use scales regularly, as weight is not important to them. Older people, too, are not so concerned about monitoring weight.

Limiting alcohol consumption to avoid alcohol-related deaths

This is another health issue that seems to be regularly newsworthy and topical. Currently, it has been re-fuelled by the extension of licensing hours for bars and public houses and by the media highlighting alcohol-related social issues, particularly 'binge drinking' among young women, many sports fans and tourists abroad. Many social commentators have compared Britain to the European continent and theorised that the UK seems to have an alcohol-culture problem that does not exist elsewhere. It is certainly of great concern to the government, health authorities and local councils. The individuals concerned appear to have no anxiety about alcohol-related illnesses and premature deaths. The same people have total disregard for safe recommended drinking levels; their only goal is to have a 'good time' and this apparently cannot happen unless they have consumed excess alcohol.

Recognising that alcohol drinking has become part of society and that group and peer pressures are difficult to resist, it is still incomprehensible that some people persist in drinking to the extent that they feel very unwell, risk chronic illness,

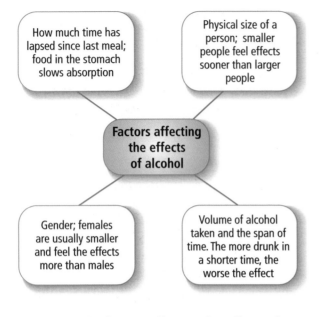

FIGURE 3.5 *The factors affecting the effects of alcohol drinking*

lose their sensibilities and even die.

The effects of alcohol drinking can be different for individuals, depending on a number of factors, as shown in Figure 3.5.

Over-consumption of alcohol produces both short-term and long-term effects; the long-term effects clearly take place over a period of several years. Table 3.2 identifies some of these effects.

People who are dependent on alcohol (alcoholics) are also likely to smoke and this increases their risks to health and well-being far more than the effects of each added together. They are also likely to suffer from malnutrition even though they appear to be of normal weight or, more likely, overweight. Like sugar, alcohol provides calories without nutrients – so-called 'empty calories'. The affection for or addiction to alcohol usually means that these individuals spend a lot of their time drinking and thus, do not take, or are incapable of, regular exercise.

Some religious groups forbid the consumption of alcohol and will be offended by questions investigating alcohol consumption.

Not smoking in order to avoid tobacco-related diseases

Like alcohol, smoking has also been very much part of society but is declining rapidly and is

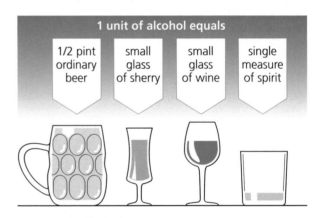

FIGURE 3.6 *Alcohol units*

considered by many to be unacceptable. One of the factors contributing to this decline is the degree of publicity that both active and passive smoking has received in relation to health risks. There has also been a number of, again, well-publicised cases of employees who have developed cancer as a result of working in smoky areas. Employers now have to provide a smoke-free healthy environment for workers. Bars, pubs and restaurants that serve food will also be required to be smoke-free in the near future by law, and many food establishments already

THE EFFECTS OF EXCESS ALCOHOL CONSUMPTION	
SHORT-TERM	**LONG-TERM**
Brain functioning is affected and errors of judgements are made, e.g. estimating distances	Very heavy drinking causes dehydration, the brain becomes inflamed and shrinks; this may lead to loss of intelligence
Although alcohol initially stimulates the mind, it is actually a depressant	Increases risks of cancer of mouth, throat, oesophagus, larynx and liver
More risks of accidents and at risk of crime attacks such as robbery, rape	Chronic liver diseases such as fatty liver and cirrhosis over several years
Loss of inhibition and more talkative; more likely to get into trouble	Nervous system disorders of walking gait, pain, cramps, tingling, etc.
Social effects, arguments, domestic violence, child abuse	Social effects, arguments, domestic violence, child abuse
Facial flushing and general dilatation of skin arteries; this can lead to exposure on very cold nights	Gastritis, pancreatitis, stomach ulcers more common
Large amounts of alcohol in a short time can lead to alcohol poisoning, a serious life-threatening condition	Anxiety, depression, dementia and suicide are more common
More urine produced (diuresis)	Increased urine produced, if prolonged can cause renal failure
Disorientation, incoherence, unconsciousness, coma, death	Increased risks of hypertension, coronary heart disease and stroke
Alcohol increases the desire for sexual intercourse but decreases the performance of it	Impotence
Slurring of speech	Foetal alcohol syndrome in pregnant women. Serious abnormalities of development can occur and low birth weight. More risk of miscarriage
Unsteady gait, risk of falls	Associated with malnutrition, particularly vitamin deficiencies. Obesity

TABLE 3.2 *Short- and long-term effects of excess alcohol consumption*

comply with this due to public demand.

The risk of lung cancer has long been known, but, until relatively recently, the risks of heart disease and other cancers were less public.

Effects of smoking on health

Some of the effects of smoking on health are shown in Figure 3.7.

Risks to health are increased in people who started smoking at a young age and in proportion to the number of cigarettes smoked.

Exercise makes people feel healthy

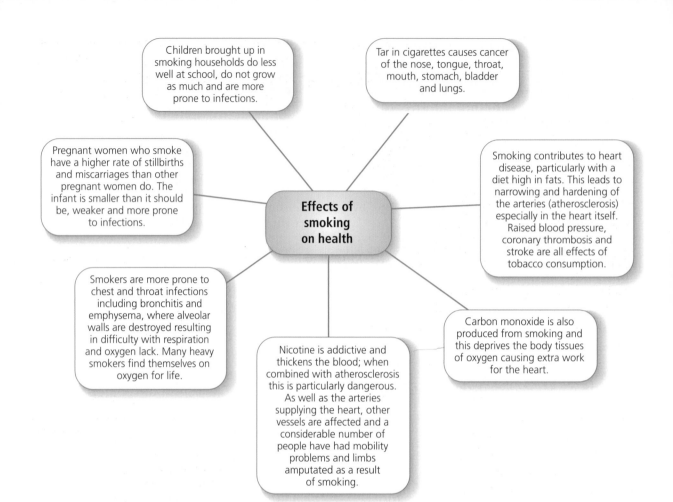

Children brought up in smoking households do less well at school, do not grow as much and are more prone to infections.

Tar in cigarettes causes cancer of the nose, tongue, throat, mouth, stomach, bladder and lungs.

Pregnant women who smoke have a higher rate of stillbirths and miscarriages than other pregnant women do. The infant is smaller than it should be, weaker and more prone to infections.

Effects of smoking on health

Smoking contributes to heart disease, particularly with a diet high in fats. This leads to narrowing and hardening of the arteries (atherosclerosis) especially in the heart itself. Raised blood pressure, coronary thrombosis and stroke are all effects of tobacco consumption.

Smokers are more prone to chest and throat infections including bronchitis and emphysema, where alveolar walls are destroyed resulting in difficulty with respiration and oxygen lack. Many heavy smokers find themselves on oxygen for life.

Nicotine is addictive and thickens the blood; when combined with atherosclerosis this is particularly dangerous. As well as the arteries supplying the heart, other vessels are affected and a considerable number of people have had mobility problems and limbs amputated as a result of smoking.

Carbon monoxide is also produced from smoking and this deprives the body tissues of oxygen causing extra work for the heart.

FIGURE 3.7 *Effects of smoking on health*

Smoking taints the taste of food so salt and other additive uses are common. Many smokers also consume alcohol as public houses and bars have been favourite meeting places. Smokers are disinclined to carry out regular exercise as they have less dissolved oxygen circulating in their blood.

Many smokers are reluctant visitors to their GP, as they know that they will be encouraged to give up and that their illness might be smoking-related.

Visiting the general practitioner to obtain medical advice and appropriately prompt treatment

At first, this might seem an obvious thing to do if you are ill – you go to the doctor!

However, many people do not visit their GP until they have had the symptoms or signs of illness for too long. Very often it is regrettably too late; the individual is seriously ill; recovery takes a long time and may not be complete. At times, there will be no recovery and death follows in due course. This is extremely sad when treatment could have been offered earlier.

Fear of being told that they have cancer or other serious illness stops many people from consulting a doctor promptly. Other people might feel that fate has intervened and that the illness is pre-destined. Many individuals consult physicians extremely rarely and are very reluctant to visit them. Smokers,

alcoholics and drug abusers tend to shy away from medical personnel. Cultures that are different from our own have varying attitudes to doctors; people may have come to live in the UK because they were oppressed and are now frightened of anyone they see 'in authority'. Women from some ethnic minorities are not allowed to speak to men that they do not know and most doctors are still male. Some religions and groups of people do not hold with blood transfusions and injections.

There is also a type of 'bureaucracy' involved in making medical appointments such as the use of the telephone early in the morning, getting past a receptionist who asks the purpose of the visit,

fitting in with work or getting time off work. These factors tend to cause people to put off making appointments, particularly timid and hesitant people or those with poor communication skills.

Summary

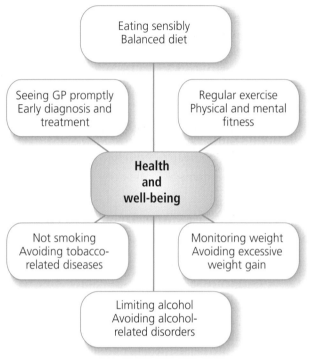

FIGURE 3.8 *Health and well-being*

Consider this

After a serious heart attack three years ago, Arthur has been referred for a heart by-pass operation and expects to have the operation next year. Unfortunately, Arthur has not yet managed to stop smoking and is still considerably overweight. He likes to go to the pub every other night to play darts with his friends and have a few pints. His doctors do not know this. Other evenings, he spends watching sport on TV. Arthur believes that his life is no different to that of his friends and thousands of others. He tells his carers that he goes for a walk each day but this tends to be only on Mondays when his pension is due and he walks about a quarter of a mile to the Post Office. Arthur regards himself as a semi-invalid and adjusts his activities to suit that view.

His wife has long since stopped complaining that he never does anything and regards him as an invalid too.

Using concepts, can you?
1 Select the factors that affect Arthur's health and well-being.

2 Explain the effects these factors are having on his health and well-being.

Going further, can you analyse issues?
3 Identify and explain how Arthur should change his lifestyle to improve his health and well-being.

4 Suggest the consequences of failing to make the changes you have identified.

Going further, can you evaluate?
5 Arthur may compromise by agreeing to walk a gently increasing distance every day. Examine the impact of one change on the inter-relationships of all the other factors.

3.3 Immunisation against disease

Immunity is the ability to resist infectious disease arising from microorganisms such as viruses, bacteria and fungi. The body can produce special proteins known as antibodies that neutralise the invading pathogens or disease-causing organisms. Immunisation – a term often used interchangeably with vaccination – is the process of artificially producing immunity by the use of a vaccine.

White blood cells are concerned with the defence of the body; lymphocytes produce antibodies and phagocytes eliminate foreign substances and antigen/antibody complexes to prevent further damage to the body.

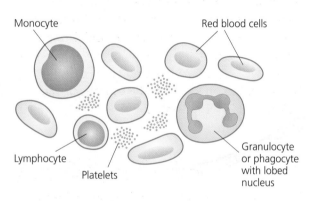

FIGURE 3.9 *Blood cells*

Pathogens have certain proteins embedded into their surfaces that are known as antigens. Antigens are generally specific to the microorganisms and have characteristic features such as shape. Antibodies have complementary shapes that attach themselves to the antigens rendering the microorganisms ineffective. The phagocytes eliminate the antigen/antibody complex. Antibodies must also be specific as they must 'fit' the antigen. In other words, the antibody for a disease like pertussis (whooping cough) is of no use in a service user with measles. Some bacteria produce poisonous proteins called toxins; these may be exotoxins that are secreted outwards or endotoxins only released when the organisms die. Clearly exotoxins produce effects quickly while endotoxins are much slower. Toxoids are inactivated

toxins used to stimulate antibody formation and are often used in vaccinations; for example, diphtheria and tetanus toxoids are constituents of DPT vaccine (see under Diphtheria).

No vaccine is known to give 100 per cent lifelong immunity to a disease.

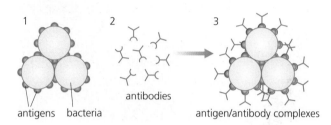

FIGURE 3.10 *Antibodies and antigens*

Innate (inborn) immunity

Each individual has a level of immunity with which they are born, known as *innate immunity*. This type of immunity consists of natural barriers to infection such as the dead, cornified layers on the outer surface of the skin, the hydrochloric acid secreted by the stomach lining, the phagocytes in blood and the lysozyme (an anti-bacterial substance) in tear fluid.

Acquired immunity

Immunity that is developed after birth is called *acquired immunity*.

Acquired immunity can be further divided into *active* and *passive types*.

Active immunity is so called because individuals produce the antibodies in the blood from their own lymphocytes. There are two ways of doing this, by *natural* means and by *artificial* methods. The immunity produced by active means is usually for a very long time, even for life; however, it takes time to develop so is of no use in giving immediate protection in an epidemic situation.

Acquired, natural active immunity

When an individual contracts a disease in the usual way from another infected person or contaminated food or water, the microorganisms multiply rapidly producing the signs and symptoms of the disease. Over a period of time the blood lymphocytes respond and begin to produce antibodies to control the infection and the individual recovers. When the person is exposed to further episodes of infection by the same microorganisms, the lymphocytes pour millions of the relevant antibodies into the blood and the progress of the disease is halted very quickly. The individual might never know that they have been in further contact with the infecting organisms or might feel a little unwell for a short period of time.

Some of these antibodies are always circulating in the blood of an individual who has recovered from a disease and there are laboratory techniques to measure the immune status of a person in this way. There has to be a certain level of specific antibodies circulating in the blood for a person to be designated 'immune'. Sometimes an individual might have a second illness of the same type, although usually milder, because their level of circulating antibodies has not been high enough to make them immune.

Acquired active artificial immunity

This is by immunisation with a vaccine. Killing the microorganisms will still leave the antigenic nature of most pathogens intact and if a sterile solution containing killed organisms is injected into an individual, it will still evoke the antibody production but without producing the effects of the disease. Two or three injections (shots or jabs) may be necessary to produce a high level of antibodies to confer immune status. In some cases, the killed vaccine is deemed to be inferior to a live, but very much weakened, dose of microorganisms. The individual may feel a little unwell with this type of vaccine but nothing as severe as the actual disease or its side effects.

Acquired passive immunity

Passive immunity occurs when the individuals have not produced the antibodies from their blood lymphocytes, and they have been introduced from elsewhere – another person or animal's blood. This means that passive immunity will confer almost immediate protection, but will not last, as the antibodies will eventually be destroyed as foreign material. Passive immunity then is useful in an epidemic or treatment situation but not as a way of providing long-term protection. There are two types of this immunity, called again *natural* and *artificial,* as shown in Table 3.3.

TYPES OF ACQUIRED PASSIVE IMMUNITY	
Acquired, natural passive immunity	The foetus in the womb will acquire maternal antibodies from the exchange across the placenta and after birth, through the mother's colostrum and breast milk. This is the main reason why mothers are urged to breastfeed a newborn infant for at least a few weeks, even if they intend to use formula milk food at a later stage. The very young infant will thus be protected against those conditions that have produced immune status in the mother. The valuable immunity received lasts only for approximately four months; thereafter, the infant is once again susceptible to diseases, so vaccination begins a little earlier to confer some degree of overlap. Note. Infants cannot receive antibodies that are not present in the mother.
Acquired, artificial passive immunity	Sometimes in epidemic situations, the authorities need to prevent further spread of a disease and can do so by providing injections of the relevant antibodies, often produced in animal bodies who themselves do not contract the disease because they are from a different species. This will provide temporary protection and hopefully stop further spread. Occasionally, antibodies are also used in treatment, particularly of an uncommon serious disease. Stocks of antiserum (serum containing antibodies) are kept in reserve for such conditions. These may have come from donated blood of individuals who have had the disease and recovered from it or from animals as described above.

TABLE 3.3 *Types of immunity*

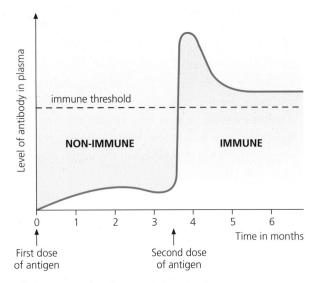

FIGURE 3.11 *How immunisation is achieved*

Some common illnesses and vaccination programmes

Diphtheria

Diphtheria is an acute bacterial illness caused by *Corynebacterium diphtheriae*; although now uncommon in developed parts of the world, it was a major cause of death in children until the 1930s.

✳ DID YOU KNOW?

Children still die from diphtheria in countries that have yet to develop good health care systems. The bacteria, carried largely in the throat or on the skin of immune people, can cause disease in non-immune persons; this is why it is of paramount importance that a high percentage of the population is immune; currently in the UK 94 per cent of the population is immune to diptheria. Some cases still occur in the UK and these are mainly among immigrants who have become carriers after a minor diphtheria infection. It is possible for immunised people to contract diphtheria but deaths are rare and the disease is mild. The disease is characterised by sore throat, lymph node enlargement of the neck and fever.

Rapid multiplication of the bacteria can lead to the formation of a membrane across the interior of the throat, often causing difficulties with air intake and a hoarse voice. The bacteria secrete a powerful exotoxin into the bloodstream and this can cause heart failure and collapse or paralysis of limb and throat muscles, so threatening life.

It is particularly important for those travelling to developing countries to have their immune status for diphtheria checked to avoid infection and to be re-immunised if warranted. One rare death in the UK occurred in a 14-year-old boy who had visited Pakistan and there appeared to be no known immunisation record. The risk is deemed by the authorities to be greater in Southeast Asia, South America, the Indian sub-continent and the former USSR.

DTP vaccination

Immunisation in infants is by three spaced injections of DPT (Diphtheria, Pertussis and Tetanus) in their first year of life. The ages at which these doses are given varies, although most commonly they are given at ages nine months, three years and five years. Approximately half a million school-leavers have also been vaccinated with DTP.

Treatment of diphtheria consists of both antibiotics (like penicillin) and antitoxin to counteract the effects of the exotoxin. Surgical opening of the airway might be necessary to overcome breathing difficulties and isolation to prevent further infection.

The installation of immunisation programmes in all countries should lead to virtual eradication of the disease.

Pertussis or whooping cough

Pertussis exists worldwide and, although it can affect adults, half the cases are in children under two years of age and those newly born are most susceptible. Infection is by airborne droplets containing the bacteria *Bordetella pertussis* being breathed in, usually from coughing. The infection results in severe inflammation of the whole respiratory tract, resulting in bouts of coughing that end in a characteristic 'whoop' or gasp. Vaccination takes place in the first year of life by DTP.

The infection can last up to three months and as it is worse at night the whole family suffers. Complications such as vomiting, dehydration, pneumonia and collapsed lung can occur.

> **✳ DID YOU KNOW?**
>
> A press campaign alerting the public to the dangers of pertussis vaccine in the 1970s caused the immune population of children to fall below 50 per cent and there were serious outbreaks of pertussis every four years. When this was later found to be a mistake, immunisation figures rose again and the incidence of the disease fell once more.

The risks of vaccination are far less than the dangers of the disease itself; the infant may develop mild fever and irritability for a day or so. Some infants, who have a fever, a history of fits or a more severe reaction to a previous dose of the vaccine, may not be given the injection. This is because about 1 per 300,000 babies may develop permanent brain damage, but the risk is very small.

Tetanus or lockjaw

The causative bacteria of this serious condition are *Clostridium tetani*, which thrive in soil, manure and intestines. They are anaerobic bacteria; this means that they thrive in poor oxygen environments. The bacteria enter the body through contaminated deep wounds such as dog bites involving the long canine teeth, pitchfork or garden fork accidents, penetrating shards of glass and even occasionally thorn pricks. In such incidents, the skin moves back over the wound leaving the bacteria deep inside in a poorly oxygenated space where they begin to multiply, producing a deadly toxin.

This toxin affects motor nerves that supply muscles, causing paralysis.

In developing countries, some infants have contracted tetanus through the umbilical cord after birth in dirty conditions.

> **✳ DID YOU KNOW?**
>
> In the UK approximately 20 cases of tetanus or lockjaw occur each year mainly in older, non-immune people. Most people recover after prompt treatment with antitoxin. People who have suffered accidents like those named above are usually given a 'booster' dose to enhance immunity if it is some years since vaccination. Ideally, people should have booster doses every ten years.

Infection results in stiffness of the jaw (hence the more common name), the facial muscles (producing a grimace), the neck, abdominal and back muscles. Asphyxia may result necessitating assisted breathing. Children are given DTP vaccination in the first year of life.

MMR (Triple) vaccine

This is a live-attenuated vaccine for measles, mumps and rubella that is given in the second year of life and again before starting school. Two doses are given at 12 and 15 months of age and at three to five years. It was developed in the early 1970s and is part of the immunisation programme in over 90 countries. In the UK there has been, and still is, a raging controversy over the safety of the vaccine to the extent that there is a government/NHS website available to the public, which gives the facts about the MMR vaccine.

Journalists regularly ask high-ranking politicians whether their own children have received the vaccine. Most decline to reply and claim privacy, but this issue does not seem to go away. The General Medical Council has issued statements, which categorically state that there is no proven link between MMR vaccination and autism or bowel disease.

Many members of the public have asked for three separate vaccinations, believing that this is a safer option. The World Health Organisation claims that the triple vaccine has an outstanding safety record and that no recommendation for separate injections is given in any country using this immunisation programme. Consequently, the government, through the NHS, declines use of separate doses of the vaccine under normal circumstances. Caution should be exercised in infants who are known to have an egg allergy, a history of fits or a positive HIV result.

One or two side effects may occur in some individuals:

* swelling of the parotid glands (salivary glands in the cheeks, mumps-like swelling)

* jerky movements particularly with walking

* pain in muscles and joints

* redness, pain and hardness at the injection site

* headache, general malaise, fever and irritability

* fits

* diarrhoea

* rash and signs of allergy.

The vaccine should not be given during pregnancy or breast-feeding.

Measles (a viral disease)

This is one of the most contagious and dangerous childhood diseases that produces a rash because of its complications. It is spread through airborne droplets, contaminated clothes, toys, etc. After an incubation period of one to two weeks, the victim complains of sore throat, cold symptoms, red eyes and coughing with a high temperature. The red rash starts near the ears and spreads to the trunk and parts of the limbs in a day or two. The individual is infectious for about four days before the rash appears, but Kopliks spots, fancifully likened to 'grains of salt on a bed of red velvet', can be seen around the molars a day or two before the rash comes.

The affected individual can be quite ill with fever, lymph gland enlargement in the neck and photophobia (dislike of light). Complications such as pneumonia, middle ear infection (otitis media) and inflammation of the nervous system can be very dangerous. Pregnant women can also be in danger. There is lifelong immunity after infection.

Mumps (a viral disease)

Mumps has a long incubation period of up to three weeks and, once again, the individual is infectious to others one week before any signs or symptoms develop, although this is the least contagious of the childhood diseases. Children between the age of one and five years are the most vulnerable, but older children and adults can contract the disease, which is spread through airborne droplets. The sufferer experiences swelling of the parotid glands on the cheeks in front of the ears, fever and difficulty opening the mouth. Some 20–30 per cent of men develop orchitis (inflammation of testes) in one or both testes and in 10 per cent of cases may become sterile in the affected organ/s. Other complications are pancreatitis (inflammation of the pancreas) and meningitis.

Rubella (a viral disease)

This mild disease, also known as German measles, is only of concern to pregnant women when it might cross the placenta in the early months and cause Rubella syndrome in the foetus.

> *** DID YOU KNOW?**
> A syndrome is a collection of signs and symptoms characteristically grouped with a distinct disease.

Spread by airborne droplets, Rubella was most common in primary school children, but through the immunisation programme, it is now less prevalent. At first, rubella vaccination was offered only to teenage girls and women planning babies and the number of cases of rubella syndrome in babies continued. Now, through the MMR vaccine, all infants are vaccinated and the number of cases has reduced.

Vaccination for travellers

Although few immunisations are compulsory for travel to countries abroad, many are advised for travellers outside Europe, North America, Australia and New Zealand.

Most UK citizens have been immunised in childhood but booster doses may be required on medical advice. Regular travellers will need to keep their immunisations up to date.

Common examples of diseases that travellers may need to be protected against are shown in Table 3.4.

EXAMPLES OF COMMON TRAVEL IMMUNISATIONS		
NATURE OF DISEASE	**WHERE?**	**EFFECTIVENESS**
Cholera (bacterial disease) from contaminated food or water, often by sewage. Produces severe, watery diarrhoea that can rapidly cause dehydration and death if untreated	Most Asian and African countries (may be compulsory immunisation in some of these countries)	Moderate protection for about six months. Bottled drinks from reliable sources should only be consumed as well
Hepatitis A (viral disease) from sewage-contaminated food and water produces a 'flu-like' illness with jaundice or may be symptomless	In countries where hygiene standards are low, particularly with respect to food hygiene	Passive immunisation is short-lived (approximately 3 months) and offers some protection. Food and personal hygiene is important
Typhoid fever (bacterial disease) major life-threatening disease causing fever, rash, diarrhoea and serious gastro-intestinal complications. Spread by contaminated food and water, flies or typhoid carriers	Most countries outside Europe, North America, Australia and New Zealand	Moderate protection for about three years (two doses recommended)
Rabies (viral disease) transmitted by a bite or lick on an open wound from a rabies-infected animal, e.g. foxes wolves, jackals, skunks and dogs. Causes a fatal inflammation of the nervous system	Very few countries are rabies-free – the UK, Scandinavia, Australia and New Zealand	Highly effective vaccine. When a bite has been given, passive immunisation is given with the least delay for treatment (limited duration)

TABLE 3.4 *Examples of common diseases that travellers may need to protect against*

Malaria

This is a disease of tropical climates, prevalent in over one hundred countries; it affects between two and three hundred million people globally each year. Malaria is spread by bites of female mosquitoes of a particular type (*Anopheles*) that carry a parasite called *Plasmodium*. The parasite spends part of its complicated life cycle in humans and part in mosquitoes, forming the most important disease hazard to people who travel to warm countries.

The disease causes severe fever and complications involving kidneys, liver, blood and brain, which can often be fatal.

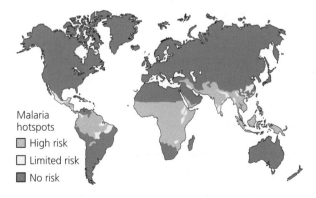

Malaria hotspots
- High risk
- Limited risk
- No risk

FIGURE 3.12 *Areas of the world where malaria occurs*

Research and development for an effective long-lasting vaccine is taking place in many clinical research facilities with varied results. However, it is not yet available for ordinary travellers who have to prepare themselves before their journey with courses of anti-malarial drugs.

Some individuals do not believe in processes like vaccination, believing that it can be more harmful than having the disease or that it is interfering with nature. Religious groups such as Jehovah's Witnesses and Christian Scientists also have different beliefs, particularly where blood transfusions and receiving blood products are concerned, although the former in recent years, have permitted vaccinations and left the matter to individual conscience. The latter believe that healing can only be spiritual by reading the words of the founder and the Bible.

Summary

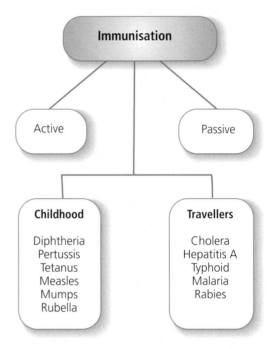

Consider this

Tania is very worried about immunisation schedules for her infant, as she has read some very scary stories in the tabloid press about immunisations causing side effects and more permanent damage such as autism. Her partner says that it is all exaggerated and to forget it. Tania cannot just dismiss these stories and it is making her very anxious. They are also planning a wonderful holiday in Kenya the following spring to show the baby to her mother-in-law who lives there.

Using concepts, can you?
1 Explain the immunisations that Tania's baby should have over the next two years.

2 Justify the vaccinations that Tania and her partner should have prior to their holiday.

Going further – can you analyse the issues?
3 Explain how immunisation works.

4 Clarify the difference between active and passive immunisation and provide examples

Going further – can you evaluate?
5 Evaluate the process of immunisation and clarify the benefits obtained.

3.4 The value of screening

Screening takes place when people are routinely tested in certain ways to aid the detection of disease at an early stage to make treatment more effective. There is no point in testing for conditions that do not respond differently when detected early. Tests for large sections of the population must be inexpensive, simple and not unpleasant for the individual. People will not attend for routine tests if put to inconvenience and discomfort. Such tests should also be reliable and accurate, not giving high figures of false positives and false negatives. These occur when the test result is judged to be different to the actual result; this has happened in the past with tests like cervical smear results, and the media are quick to highlight such errors.

Nevertheless, screening provides valuable information that protects the health of different client groups and saves many lives. The first screening tests occur even before birth, as a part of antenatal care of pregnant women.

Antenatal screening tests

Two membranes surround the developing embryo, the amnion and the chorion; the amnion also known as the amniotic sac is a bag-like structure containing the embryo and amniotic fluid. As development proceeds, foetal skin cells are shed into the fluid and certain chemicals accumulate there. The chorion further develops into the placenta, which consists of microscopical projections of tissue containing loops of foetal blood capillaries (chorionic villi) lying in small 'lakes' of maternal blood. Small molecular materials can pass to and fro between these two blood streams across the intervening delicate membranes, although the actual blood does not mix. Amniocentesis and chorionic villus sampling are usually undertaken when special blood tests have revealed 'markers' or pointers for genetic disorders and when there is evidence of advancing maternal age. These blood serum markers are alphafetoprotein, human chorionic gonadotrophin, oestriol and inhibinA; a pointer from ultrasound scanning of nuchal translucency can be used as well. A foetus with Down's

syndrome has a thicker layer of amniotic fluid at the base of the neck resulting in different translucency (the amount of light permitted to pass through).

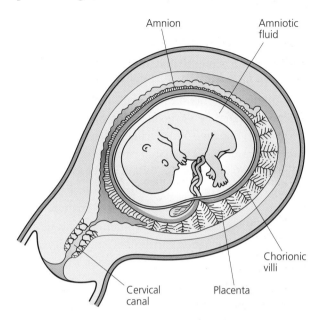

FIGURE 3.13 *A foetus*

Chorionic villus sampling (CVS)

This can be performed earlier than amniocentesis, within the first 12 weeks or later. The test is used where there is a family history of a genetic abnormality or the individual is deemed to be of special risk of inheriting such an abnormality. The cells of the chorionic villi have the same genetic make-up as the foetus and, after removal, are grown in a culture medium so that the chromosomes can be analysed.

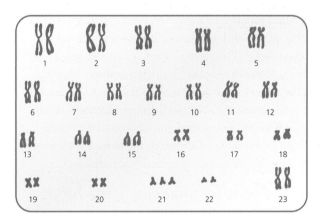

FIGURE 3.14 *Karyogram showing 3 chromosomes at position 21 – Down's syndrome*

Typical genetic abnormalities investigated using CVS are Down's syndrome, haemophilia, thalassaemia, muscular dystrophy and sickle cell disorders.

The test is usually carried out as an outpatient and takes about 30 minutes. The sample can be obtained from the foetal side of the edge of the placenta by a cannula (thin, hollow tube) attached to a syringe. Access is either through the vagina and uterus or the abdominal wall. The former method is aided by using an endoscope (an instrument used for direct visual access of a hollow organ or cavity) and the latter by an ultrasound scan to locate the placenta. When evidence of a serious chromosome abnormality is found, the parents can be given the choice of termination or not. The advantages of CVS over amniocentesis are that earlier termination carries less emotional stress and less risk to the health of the mother.

Risks of CVS are:

✳ puncturing the amniotic sac

✳ bleeding

✳ infection.

There is also a 1–2 per cent increased risk of miscarriage.

Amniocentesis

Small amounts of amniotic fluid are withdrawn from the amniotic sac for skin cell culture and chemical analysis. The technique is performed during the sixteenth and eighteenth week of the pregnancy, and the positions of the foetus and placenta are located by ultrasound scanning to allow the free passage of a hollow needle to remove a small amount of fluid. The needle penetrates the abdominal and uterine walls with local or no anaesthetic. There is a slightly increased risk (1 per cent) of miscarriage with this procedure. Results take three to four weeks, as cells have to be grown for chromosome analysis. Alphafetoprotein levels and foetal blood groups can also be determined from amniotic fluid although the main function is to investigate chromosomal abnormalities.

Blood tests for anaemia, spina bifida and blood groupings

The mother's blood provides vital dissolved oxygen for the growing foetus and this exchange takes place across the placenta (see Antenatal screening on page 121). When the mother is anaemic, that is her blood has a lack of oxygen-carrying capacity, most probably due to iron deficiency, then her foetus will not receive the desired supply of oxygen for its needs. The baby will be small for date and function might be impaired. A sample of blood taken from a vein in the forearm will enable laboratory determination of the level of iron-containing haemoglobin in the red blood cells.

When this is deemed to be inadequate, the pregnant mother can be provided with relevant medication. At the same time, testing against specific antisera assesses the mother's blood group; the blood group may be important if, as happens rarely, complications develop necessitating blood transfusion. In a small number of cases, the mother and foetus may have incompatible blood groups and, although the two bloods do not actually mix, some special precautions may have to be taken, especially at birth.

When a mother has Rhesus negative (D -ve) blood and the foetus Rhesus positive (D +ve) blood, the first foetus may sensitise the mother by causing Rhesus antibodies to develop. This usually happens during the birth as the placenta is breaking away from the uterine wall. An injection of anti-D serum will 'mop up' the antibodies, and prevent sensitisation. This is necessary because in a second or subsequent pregnancy with a Rhesus positive baby, the mother's antibodies will start to destroy the blood of the foetus, causing severe jaundice and even death.

Blood levels of certain chemicals will also provide pointers to other risks such as spina bifida, which causes high levels of alphafetoprotein.

Infant and child screening tests

Blood tests for CH, PKU and thalassaemia

After the infant is born, certain screening tests are carried out to ensure that the child is not affected by detectable conditions that were not apparent during antenatal care.

Congenital hypothyroidism (used to be called cretinism, now more commonly referred to as CH) and phenylketonuria (called PKU) are conditions that should never be missed, as both seriously affect growth and development – particularly mental development – and both are treatable conditions.

PKU is tested by a small prick on the heel of an infant and the drop of blood produced is mopped up on to a specially treated card. This is known as the Guthrie test and looks for high levels of phenylalanine that the infant is unable to metabolise due to a genetic inborn error of metabolism. The infants are usually blue-eyed and have blonde hair, as melanin is unable to be produced from the phenylalanine, although this is often difficult to tell in the newly born.

Thalassaemia is an inherited blood disorder and is most common in families originally from the Mediterranean area, South East Asia and the Middle East. Red blood cells are easily broken and are pale, due to a fault in haemoglobin manufacture. The infant and child will thus suffer from anaemia and insufficient oxygen carriage. A microscopic analysis of blood and haemoglobin estimation will diagnose this condition.

> ## ✳ DID YOU KNOW?
>
> As the UK becomes increasingly multicultural and mixed race unions are common, an increasing number of cases of thalassaemia, sickle cell anaemia and other blood disorders now occur. There are moves to make these blood tests part of routine infant care throughout the whole of the UK. This already occurs in some geographical areas of Britain, where there are large numbers of people from the countries mentioned.

Dental examination for dental caries

Children should have regular examinations of their milk or deciduous teeth from an early age so that monitoring for dental caries (decay) and the formation of the permanent teeth can be carried out. At the same time, advice regarding good personal mouth hygiene can be given. The dentist will examine and record the status of each tooth using a mirror and probe.

Currently, depending on the individual and the health status of the teeth, the dentist will determine the interval between examinations;

although this used to be half-yearly, the shortage of dentists working for the NHS has determined re-planning. In some areas, there are no NHS dentists and the community is experiencing much longer delays.

Eye tests for visual defects

A health professional will observe whether the baby looks at the mother when feeding and in many areas a pupillary red reflex test is carried out using an ophthalmoscope (a special instrument for looking into the eye. Most people will have seen flash photographs where the flash has illuminated the back of the eye, causing the person to have red eyes. This is essentially the same principle as using the ophthalmoscope. When an infant or child has congenital cataracts the red-eye reflex is absent.

The pupil reaction to light test is also carried out. When a bright light is shone on to the pupil of the eye, the pupil becomes smaller and vice versa in dim light conditions. When the infant is six to eight weeks old, the mother is asked for her opinion regarding the infant's eyesight, the red reflex test is again carried out and the observer notes the fixation of the eyes on the mother's face.

FIGURE 3.15 *The Sheridan-Gardner test being carried out*

At the eight-month check, the infant should follow moving objects and be able to focus on and reach out for a small object.

The child is assessed for squint at each eye test from this stage. At three years of age, visual acuity is measured using a letter-matching chart with the observer showing single letters and asking the child to point out a matching letter (Sheridan-Gardner test, see Figure 3.15).

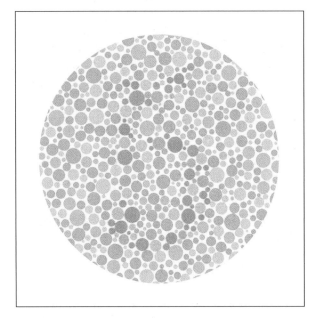

FIGURE 3.16 *An Ishihara chart*

At school, the familiar Snellen chart with letters of different sizes is used to test visual acuity. Near vision, colour vision (Ishihara charts (see Figure 3.16) or wool) and myopia (short-sightedness) are also tested for.

Hearing tests for deafness

In the UK about 700 children are discovered to have severely impaired hearing each year. Early treatment leads to improved language skills and fewer emotional problems. However, like visual tests, there is much controversy over current hearing tests and these may be replaced in time with some form of electronic tests that may be more reliable and quantitative. Infants are observed for their reactions to noise, particularly voices. Babies will usually quieten in these conditions. From eight months onwards, infants will first move their heads sideways to locate noise and a little later up and down movements are added, giving full rotating head movement towards sound. This is used in distraction testing – various noises, like a shaken rattle, siren or whistle, are made in different locations to watch if the infant turns the head to the sound. After a child's second birthday, word-object testing is used; the care professional whispers the name of an object and asks the child to point to it.

Word-object testing is used to check hearing

A further test requests the child to carry out a particular task when certain sounds are made. It is also important to listen to the mother's views on the ability of the child to hear well, such as reaction to television sound, a doorbell ringing, or a dog barking and so on. If there is any doubt about the child's hearing, specialist advice is sought.

Physical examination for hip dislocation

The femur is the longest and strongest bone in the body; the head is a round ball that fits snugly in a cup-shaped depression in the pelvis. Sometimes the cup is not deep enough to hold the femoral head and it moves outwards, so-called dislocation. Some infants are born with permanent dislocated hips (one or both). This condition has been re-named developmental dysplasia of the hip, or DDH for short. When the condition is not discovered for some time, the child may walk with a painless limp, but osteo-arthritis of the joint occurs much earlier in life than normal and the hip joint becomes very painful. With early diagnosis and treatment, there is no limp and no early onset of osteo-arthritis.

The physical examination should take place at birth, at six to eight weeks old, and six to eight months. With the infant lying on its back, the doctor flexes the hip and knee to 90° vertically, with the thumb on the inner side of the knee and the forefinger on the outer bump of the head of the femur, the hip is turned smoothly and gently outwards (see Figure 3.17). When the hip joint is unstable there is a 'clunk' that can be both felt and heard as the head of the femur slips out of the socket (acetabulum) on the pelvis. Each hip is examined separately. The absence of the 'clunk' indicates that the hip joints are stable.

Recent research studies have demonstrated that two out of three of cases of children requiring

surgery at a later date for this condition were not 'picked up' by this test. This has caused great concern and moves are being made to add to or replace this test by ultrasound scanning.

> ### ✳ DID YOU KNOW?
>
> One of the main problems of DDH examination is that newly born infants are frequently affected by a hormone circulating in pregnant mothers and this makes their ligaments slack. Infant musculature is also weak and these two factors can cause unstable hips that clear up without any treatment. More than one in 100 infants born have unstable hip joints. Interestingly, DDH is six times more common in girls, and the left hip is affected four times more than the right hip. In one to three of the cases in which both hips are affected, there is a family history of the condition.

Treatment is by splints, plaster casts or surgery if this fails.

Adult screening tests

Screening tests may be suitable for the whole population, such as those for infants and children; however, others may be applicable to groups of people at special risk such as a particular age group or gender, certain hazardous occupations or those with family histories of disease.

Blood pressure tests for hypertension

Increasingly, more young adults are affected by a higher resting blood pressure than normal (hypertension) whereas the condition used to be thought of as relevant only to middle-aged and older people. GPs are urged to routinely measure blood pressures of service users on visits to the surgery. Other clients are urged to visit the practice at least once a year to have their blood pressure checked. Clients with hypertension, or raised blood pressure not yet deemed to be clinical hypertension, are advised to attend regular clinics for monitoring purposes. Hypertension increases the chances of life-threatening conditions such as strokes and heart disease, particularly coronary thrombosis.

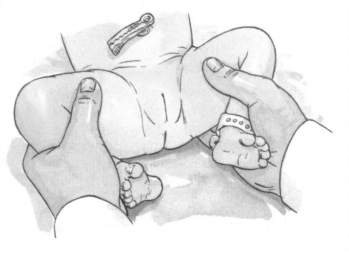

FIGURE 3.17 *Testing a baby for hip displacement*

It is normal to experience raised blood pressure during periods of stress or physical exertion. Hypertension is raised blood pressure at rest. Blood pressure rises naturally with age because of hardening and narrowing of the elastic arteries. It also rises with kidney disease, narrowing of the aorta (the main artery serving the body), alcohol consumption, smoking tobacco products and hormonal disorders. Pregnant women may experience raised blood pressure in a serious condition known as pre-eclampsia.

Nowadays, blood pressure is usually measured electronically as the old mercury devices are banned. A device for measuring blood pressure is called a sphygmomanometer or 'sphygmo' for short and is usually used on the upper arm over the position of an artery. An inflatable cuff is blown up to stop the blood flowing through the artery and slowly deflated until the point is reached when blood is just able to push through. This is the systolic pressure and represents the force, which the blood is pressing on the artery walls, when the heart ventricles are contracting (systole).

The cuff is further deflated until blood is first flowing naturally and the heartbeat disappears; this is the diastolic pressure measuring the resistance of the arteries against which the heart has to pump blood. This is seen as the most important reading, as the systolic pressure is frequently raised due to excitement, anxiety or physical exertion. Individuals should sit quietly for about ten minutes before having their blood pressure recorded. The two, recorded pressures are usually given as a fraction with the larger systolic as the numerator and the diastolic as the denominator. The first instruments measured in millimetres of mercury (mm.Hg) and this is still the most frequently used unit, although units are frequently omitted; thus BP 120/80.

Most normal healthy young people have blood pressures around 110/75 or even less, although the average normal BP is quoted at 120/80.

Hypertension is quoted to be BP consistently over 160/95 mm.Hg, but there is no absolute line and many individuals with borderline hypertension are carefully monitored by their GP and advised accordingly. Males are more frequently affected with hypertension than females and for many individuals there appears to be no underlying cause. Clinical investigation for any underlying cause is carried out and anti-hypertensive drugs are effective in lowering blood pressure.

Smear test for cervical cancer

This is a test recommended that women take six months after first sexual intercourse, then after one year and every three years, ideally until the end of their lives. In the UK at present, cervical smear tests cease at the age of sixty-five years unless there is a particular reason for continuing monitoring. The test detects abnormal cells in the cervix or neck of the womb. Abnormal cells usually indicate a pre-cancerous condition and the smear test has a 95 per cent chance of detecting these. Cancer of the cervix is one of the most common cancers in the world and the chances of a cure are very much improved with early detection. Herpes simplex (a troublesome virus infection) and genital warts can also be detected.

A woman lies on her back, with knees raised and pressed open, and an instrument (speculum) opens the vagina so that a specially shaped spatula can be inserted to scrape off some cells to be smeared on to a microscope slide. The quick test is carried out in family planning and well woman clinics, or by a GP, but the results are not routinely ready for several weeks. When abnormal cells are found, the test is usually repeated and the abnormality graded by experts. Sometimes a biopsy (removal of a small piece of tissue) is carried out to determine the extent and full nature of the abnormality. When the area of abnormality is well defined this can be eradicated and destroyed by extreme heat or cold. The cervical smear test is free under the NHS.

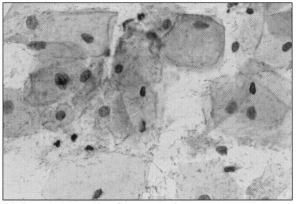

Light micrograph of a cervical smear containing normal squamous cells (pink and blue) and numerous rod-shaped bacteria

Eye tests for glaucoma and other visual defects

Some of the titles used by eye professionals are confusing and it is important to understand the different terms.

Ophthalmologists are doctors who specialise in eye disorders and treatment; ophthalmic opticians are trained to perform eye examinations and prescribe glasses to correct visual defects.

Ophthalmic opticians are not doctors who treat eye disorders and will refer any concerns in this regard to ophthalmologists. Opticians fit and sell glasses. It follows then, that the professional (other than a doctor) who might carry out a routine eye examination should be an ophthalmic optician and not an optician,

The eyeball is fluid-filled to enable the shape of the eye to be maintained. The volume of fluid entering the eye must balance with the volume leaving the eye; in glaucoma, the exit of fluid is narrowed so more fluid enters than leaves, causing the pressure inside the eyeball to rise.

A raised intra-ocular pressure damages the optic nerve at the back of the eye, causing patchy loss of vision. The extent of visual loss depends on the type of glaucoma and how long the raised pressure has been undiagnosed. When intra-ocular pressure is monitored regularly, damage will be minimised. This is important because any long-standing damage will cause the visual loss to be permanent. The individual will not necessarily be aware of the patchy vision because most tasks are carried out by central vision, such as reading and watching television, for example, and central vision only becomes affected at a later stage in glaucoma.

Glaucoma usually affects both eyes. Individuals over the age of 40 years are generally tested regularly; those with a family history of the condition from thirty-five years of age, but Afro-Caribbean people, diabetics, people with myopia and heavy smokers should be tested earlier, as glaucoma is significantly more common in these groups.

An applanation tonometer is used to measure the intra-ocular pressure, a specialist piece of equipment. The ophthalmoscope is also used to examine the back of the eye where the optic nerve disc can be viewed.

Measurement of visual fields can also be important for checking on peripheral vision and clearly the accuracy of vision using Snellen charts is vital (see eye tests in children on page 124).

> ### ✱ DID YOU KNOW?
>
> Glaucoma is responsible for 15 per cent of blindness in adults in the UK and is the most common major eye disorder in people over 60 years of age.

Astigmatism is a 'bumpy' cornea that causes some parts of vision to be clearer than others are;

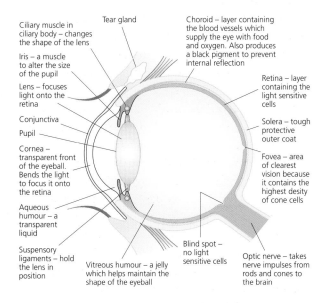

Ciliary muscle in ciliary body – changes the shape of the lens

Iris – a muscle to alter the size of the pupil

Lens – focuses light onto the retina

Conjunctiva

Pupil

Cornea – transparent front of the eyeball. Bends the light to focus it onto the retina

Aqueous humour – a transparent liquid

Suspensory ligaments – hold the lens in position

Tear gland

Choroid – layer containing the blood vessels which supply the eye with food and oxygen. Also produces a black pigment to prevent internal reflection

Retina – layer containing the light sensitive cells

Solera – tough protective outer coat

Fovea – area of clearest vision because it contains the highest desity of cone cells

Blind spot – no light sensitive cells

Vitreous humour – a jelly which helps maintain the shape of the eyeball

Optic nerve – takes nerve impulses from rods and cones to the brain

FIGURE 3.18 *A section through the eyeball*

it is often tested for using a series of black lines arranged as spokes of a wheel on green and red backgrounds. Some spokes appear blacker than others do. Corrective lenses in glasses are able to cancel the effect out.

Myopia (short-sight), hypermetropia (long-sight) and presbyopia (long-sight of old age) are investigated using trial spectacles into which loose lenses can be placed until vision is near perfect.

Mammography for breast cancer

This is an X-ray procedure for screening for breast cancer and lumps. Like the cervical smear test, mammography can reveal small lumps that are not apparent to touch even if the women practices breast self-examination; and early diagnosis is an important factor in the reduction of fatalities from this disease. Each breast in turn is gently compressed between a plastic plate and the X-ray plate to spread the tissue over a wide area. Views are taken in more than one plane. Specialists inspect the X-ray photographs looking for dense masses of tissue. When a lump is found, a biopsy is arranged to determine further treatment. Currently, most small tumours are surgically removed and combined with radiotherapy and/or anti-cancer drugs.

Mammography is available as routine screening for anyone aged 40 with a family history of the disease and, for other women, from 50 until 65 years. It is simple, safe (uses only a low dose of radiation) and effective. Screening

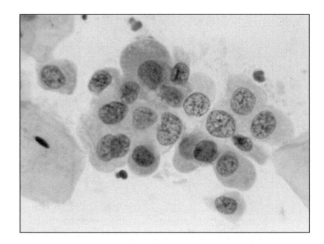

should be repeated every three or four years, as this is the most common cancer in women. Mammography is free under the NHS.

Physical examination for testicular cancer

Testicular cancer is rare in puberty and old age; conversely it is most common in young adults and middle-aged men. Both testes should be regularly felt over the whole surface, moving the loose skin of the scrotum from side to side. It is easy and simple to do and should not cause discomfort. Any firm lumps, not usually painful or tender, should be followed up promptly by the GP, who will treat any lump as malignant (invasive) until proven otherwise. Testicular cancer has an extremely good cure rate when caught in the early stages.

Summary

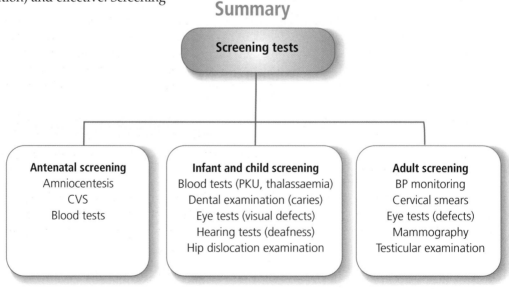

```
                    Screening tests

  Antenatal screening    Infant and child screening    Adult screening
  Amniocentesis          Blood tests (PKU, thalassaemia)  BP monitoring
  CVS                    Dental examination (caries)    Cervical smears
  Blood tests            Eye tests (visual defects)     Eye tests (defects)
                         Hearing tests (deafness)       Mammography
                         Hip dislocation examination    Testicular examination
```

Tania has just learned that she is pregnant with her first child; both she and her partner are very happy, as they have been wanting to start a family for a year. Tania is 39 years old, and five years ago had a small lump removed from her left breast. The lump was discovered after a routine mammography. She also has had cervical smears every three years, all of which have been negative. Her blood group is Rhesus negative and her partner is Rhesus positive, and she has had mild iron-deficiency anaemia for most of her adult life due to heavy menstrual periods.

Tania has had annual eye tests because she is short-sighted and astigmatic. Her older sister has four children and began her family when she was 23 years old. She has three girls and one boy, the youngest, has Down's syndrome.

Using concepts, can you identify?

1 The antenatal screening tests that Tania would be advised to have by her health care advisors.

2 The screening tests her newly born infant will have.

3 The adult screening tests that Tania has experienced.

Go further – can you analyse issues using theory?

4 The scientific basis for each of the antenatal, infant and adult tests you have named.

5 How positive and negative results would be obtained for each screening test.

Go further – can you evaluate using a range of theory?

6 Explain the values of the screening tests to the health of Tania and her baby.

UNIT 3 ASSESSMENT

You will need to produce a portfolio of evidence containing a questionnaire and two reports. The work should be wholly your own work and not shared with other candidates or part of a group exercise.

A: The Questionnaire

You will need to construct a sound questionnaire to demonstrate the differing attitudes to the concept of health and ill health and to determine how the understanding of people is different. Further questions should then examine all the factors affecting health and well-being, focusing on their relative importance, the reasons for them and how they link into one another.

You will need to decide on the number of people to be surveyed by the questionnaire and include as many different individuals and groups of people of different culture, beliefs and settings as you can. Your questionnaire should be designed so that when you collate the responses you can analyse the results and provide evidence showing how you assessed the validity and accuracy of the data that you have collected. You will need to draw conclusions from your survey and justify how you reached those conclusions.

✳ DID YOU KNOW?

Questionnaires are an effective way to gather information on people's thoughts, views or activities; however, they need to be carefully designed and planned.

First of all, make sure that you are fully briefed on the topic and while you are doing your research, jot down any ideas on possible questions to ask. At this stage, do not try to write the question because you may decide on a special format later, just a note will do. When your research is concluded, check whether you have covered all the aspects required.

Decide on the breadth of your survey, by considering the number of people you will question, who these will be and where you can find different people from different groups of society. You will also need to consider how many questionnaires will be returned and increase your number to offset the shortfall. For example, if after careful consideration, you think that you will survey 50 people in total and there will be 1 in 5 who will not complete the questionnaire, then you will need to increase the number of people surveyed to 60.

The style of the questionnaire is important, as it can make the difference between getting it completed or not, so you should bear in mind the people who will be answering it. The questionnaire should not be too long and make people give up, or so short that you have too little material to analyse. Design your questions so that there is a mix of different formats with not too much writing; short answer questions and boxes for completion are good. A brief introduction giving the purpose of the request is useful, particularly if you plan not to give out each questionnaire yourself.

It is useful to give the questionnaire to an individual and provide a short time interval for completion. If you hover over someone while they are completing the questionnaire, you are less likely to get honest and detailed responses. You will also need to consider how the completed questionnaires will be returned to you.

✳ DID YOU KNOW?

Questions can be in different formats. When seeking an opinion or view, you can ask an open question (often beginning with what, how, why, where or when) such as:

What does being healthy mean to you?
Responders would need a few lines for their answer. Open questions are more difficult to answer because, hopefully, the answer is more detailed and considered.

When you are seeking facts, you are more likely to ask closed questions; these require yes or no answers or just a simple fact such as:

Have you seen a doctor for advice or treatment in the last six months?   Yes/No
In this case you can provide options for the responder to use by circling, ticking or underlining the correct answer. You will need to provide the instruction for completion, such as 'please circle your answer'.

You can also provide a small number of choices to limit the response types. This makes analysis easier for you, but also can be frustrating for the individual if the response they wish to give is not available.

How many times have you seen a doctor for advice and/or treatment in the past twelve months?
Please tick one box only

None ☐   Once ☐   2–3 times ☐   4–8 times ☐   more than 8 times ☐

You can also use restricted options to simplify responses for analysis by making a statement and asking for agreement or disagreement. This is a verbal rating scale.

All tobacco products should be banned from public places immediately.

Please tick one box only

Strongly agree   ☐
Agree   ☐
Neither agree nor disagree   ☐
Disagree   ☐
Strongly disagree   ☐

You can also use ranking questions, asking the responder to rank a list in order of importance, such as:

Please rank the following in order of importance to your health.

(1 = most important, 6 = least important.)

Eating sensibly ☐

Regular exercise or physical activity ☐

Monitoring your weight ☐

Limiting alcohol consumption ☐

Avoiding smoking ☐

Visiting the GP promptly for medical advice and appropriate treatment ☐

Another way of gauging opinion is to use a graded scale on which the responder makes a judgement, such as:

Estimate your health status by placing a mark in the appropriate place on the line below:

|_____|

Not healthy   Full health

You will need to consider your notes and decide which format is most suitable to investigate the questions you wish to ask. When you have written your questions in your desired format, it is worth carrying out a small trial to test whether the questionnaire 'works' and whether adjustments need to be made. At this stage, it will be useful to consider how you will collate and analyse your results in order to achieve high marks. Careful planning now will save hours of work later on.

You are recommended to make regular perusals of the assessment objectives and marking grids to maximise your achievement. For example, when using a graded question like the one above, you may wish to have a copy with divisions marked on so that you can place it over the response and transfer to a percentage or number for collation purposes.

B: Report 1

This report assesses your understanding of the Immunisation against Disease part of the specification. You will need to carry out original research to accurately explain the rationale behind both active and passive immunity. Each listed disease should be covered by a brief description of aetiology (study of the causes), signs and symptoms and the importance of immunisation to prevent specific long-term damage. You will also need to evaluate immunisation against non-immunisation and include a consideration of the side effects of immunisation. To gain high marks, you will need to provide depth and breadth of understanding in your report, use a variety of research sources and different contexts.

You are recommended to make regular perusals of the assessment objectives and marking grids to maximise your achievement.

C: Report 2

The second report assesses the Value of Screening section of the specifications. The report should explain the value of screening for different client groups. Each screening test should be briefly described, including the way in which it is performed and how results are interpreted. Clearly referenced research resources from a variety of sources should explain the scientific basis of the test and the results obtained from it. To gain high marks, you must show depth and breadth of understanding of the importance of screening tests for different client groups and stress the scientific principles underlying each test.

You are recommended to make regular perusals of the assessment objectives and marking grids to maximise your achievement.

References

Any good health or medical encyclopaedia will have details of screening tests.

Aggleton, P., (1990) *Health (Society Now)*, Routledge, London

British Medical Association, (2000) *Complete Family Health Encyclopedia*, Dorling Kindersley, London

Ewles, L., Simnett, I., (2003) *Promoting Health – a Practical Guide*, Bailliere Tindall, London.

Kassianos, G. C., (2001) *Immunization: Childhood and Traveller's Health*, Blackwell Science, Oxford

Naidoo, J., (1997) *Health Studies: An Introduction*, Palgrave Macmillan, Basingstoke

Neustaedter, R., (2002) *The Vaccine Guide: Risks and Benefits for Children and Benefits*, North Atlantic Books, Berkley, California

Neustaedter, R., (1990) *The Immunization Decision: A Guide for Parents*, North Atlantic Books, Berkley, California

Romm, A. J., (2001) *Vaccinations: A Thoughtful Parent's Guide*, Healing Arts Press, Rochester, New York

Seedhouse, D., (1986) *Health: The Foundations for Achievement*, John Wiley, Chichester

Senior, M., Viveash, B., (1997) *Skills-based Sociology*, Macmillan, London

Taylor, S., Field, D., (1998) *Sociological Perspectives on Health, Illness and Healthcare*, Blackwell Science, Oxford

Useful websites

Please see www.heinemann.co.uk/hotlinks (express code 1562P) for links to the following websites which may provide a source of information:

* The Department of Health and Human Services has a website of Centres for Disease Control and Prevention.

* The NHS Immunisation information site provides information on MMR.

* Trekmate is an outdoor and store which carries trekking and extreme weather equipment for sale or rent.

* The Association for Clinical Biochemistry and the American Association of Clinical Chemistry has a non-commercial lab tests online site.

* The website of the UK government has information on disabilities and many other topics.

* Surgery Door provides an online health service.

Answers to assessment questions

Unit 1

1. Find out, or be given information about, their treatment, future opportunities or prospects.

   * Be given coherent explanations for their condition and future treatment.

   * Ask questions and receive answers.

   * Be listened to.

2. Distraction is a caring technique often used for a service user in constant pain. It can be used when medication is wearing off and the next cannot yet be given or if time is required for the medication to work. Some people are able to distract themselves successfully and other methods require a good rapport between the service user and the carer. One type utilises external material such as books, paintings or music while the other uses the imagination such as being in a pleasantly familiar place or imagining lying on a beach in the warm sunshine, or skiing in the snow. Distraction does not mean there is still no pain but the mind is able to shut down the pain to varied degrees by concentrating on other things.

3. Setting challenges for any service user is a foundation for making progress providing that the challenge is achievable and worth doing. No one likes being set something that they view as utterly pointless, particularly an older person. If the benefits of the challenge are clearly motivating, it is more likely to be successful. An older service user who is recovering from a hip replacement operation may have the view that he or she needs to spend all day in bed resting; encouraging this individual to be more mobile, in small steps, will avoid sometimes life-threatening complications such as deep vein thrombosis. It will also prevent further muscle deterioration and stimulate the appetite so that the right

foods are eaten to assist healing. Achieving improvements in circulation and respiration will follow movements and help to prevent fluid accumulation. Running alongside the challenges is working alongside – accompanying the service user for each short walk and showing approval as the challenges are met. The service user will usually look forward to returning home and this is likely to be achieved sooner if individual challenges are given and met.

4. Confidentiality. Try to establish if the man is really who he says he is – perhaps by asking relevant questions that only the next of kin would know. Refuse to give out any information on the phone even thought to be the enquiry is genuine. Call a senior member of staff to take the call or ask for a number so that his call can be returned.

5. Mr B loves his wife and is concerned for her welfare. He feels that other service users' needs are being met before those of his wife. He feels helpless and this is making him very angry because he is used to protecting his family from distress and trauma. It is unacceptable to have an operation cancelled three times but regrettably this does happen. Clearly, you should inform a supervisor as soon as possible about Mr B's fury and aggressive attitude. Mr B is upsetting other service users as well, so the first thing to do is to ask him to come into a quiet room. If he refuses, calmly and quietly explain that your supervisor will speak with him shortly if he calms down and if he is not going to listen, then you must call security. You should know where the alarms are and whether other staff are around. Place yourself in front of Mr B with your back to the exit. Explain to Mr B that you will make your request once more and then leave to get a supervisor, shout for help or sound the alarm. On no account

E

Effective communication: This enables a person to access information they need by asking questions, being listened to and being given coherent explanations.

Empowerment: Being given power. Not being dependent on others – taking control of own life decisions.

Endoscopy: A procedure for placing a thin, lighted tube down an orifice to visually examine a tube or cavity.

Endotoxin: A poison produced within pathogens.

Equitable treatment: Receiving treatment which might not be the same as the treatment of others but is likely to be seen as fair and not significantly better or worse.

Evaluation: To evaluate something is to assess it, in particular its worth, value or importance.

Exotoxin: A poison produced externally by pathogens.

F

Facilitator: A person who helps to make something happen. This is often associated with decision-making or planning.

G

Group maintenance: The social needs of group members when they are working. Maintenance activities create an appropriate social atmosphere to enable members to work effectively.

Group task: The work or activities that a group of people have come together to do.

H

Holism: Affecting the whole person not a part.

Hypertension: Raised resting blood pressure, usually above 160/95 mmHg.

I

Illness: A subjective sensation of being unwell.

Immunity: Defence against disease.

Innate immunity: Natural defences from birth.

L

Lymphocytes: White blood cells that produce antibodies.

M

Maladaptive behaviour: Behaviour that is not appropriate to the needs of local or general society.

Makaton: A system for developing language that uses speech, signs and symbols to help people with learning difficulties to communicate and to develop their language skills.

Modelling: Using socially acceptable behaviour as a role model for others in the hope that an individual will start to copy that behaviour

MRSA: Methicillin-resistant *Staphylococcus aureus* – a bacterial infection that develops in hospital environments, causing death or complications in vulnerable people.

N

Natural immunity: Immunity that occurs through natural causes such as recovering from infection or passing from mother to foetus through the placenta.

Needlestick injury: The accidental insertion of a syringe needle into the skin of a person not designated to receive it, usually a carer.

Neglect: A lack of attention and due care which might result in physical or psychological harm to a service user.

Norms: The expectations that people have of other people within a particular group or culture – what people regard as normal.

Nuchal translucency: Examining the degree of light shining through the amniotic fluid at the base of the neck (used in investigations related to Down's syndrome).

O

Occupation: Having something interesting or worthwhile to do, either a job or hobby.

Open question: A question to which the respondent replies in his or her own words. Such questions cannot usually be answered by a simple 'yes' or 'no'.

Ophthalmoscope: An instrument with lenses and a strong light for examining the back of the eyeball.

P

Paraphrase: To put what you think a person has said into your own words.

Passive immunity: Immunity that results from antibodies being introduced into the body.

Pathogens: Disease-causing micro-organisms.

Person centred planning: A way of working with people with learning disabilities. This was promoted by a government initiative called Valuing People. It includes the service user, his or her family, carer(s) and friends in the care planning and management process, together with professionals from the relevant services.

Privacy: Opportunities to be undisturbed or unobserved by others in situations likely to cause embarrassment.

Probes and prompts: A probe is a very short question that is used to 'dig deeper' or probe into a person's answer. Prompts are short questions or words, which you offer to the other person in order to prompt them to answer.

Psychological security: The absence of fear or distressing anxiety.

Q

Qualitative data: Data that cannot be expressed in numerical form. It is often about attitudes, opinions and values.

Quantitative data: Data which is expressed in numerical form.

R

Reductionism: Examining only the part of the body that is not functioning correctly.

Reflection: Thinking back over your actions.

S

Self-advocacy: Speaking up for yourself to make sure that your views and wishes are heard.

Self-directed support: A process that involves the service user in playing a key role in decision-making about the services that he or she wants.

Self-esteem: How well or how badly a person feels about himself or herself. High self-esteem may help a person to feel happy and confident. Low self-esteem may lead to depression and unhappiness.

Semi-structured data: Information collected about specified topics, but expressed in the respondents' own words.

Social contact: Opportunities to be with other people.

Social perception: Recognition of a service user's feelings, needs and intentions.

Social support: Opportunities to be with familiar and trusted people who act in a service user's best interests.

Speech communities: A speech community might be based on people who live in a geographical area, a specific ethnic group, or different professions and work cultures. Speech communities are evidenced by their own special words, phrases and speech patterns.

Stereotyping: A fixed way of thinking involving generalisations and expectations about issues or a group of people.

Stimulation: The presence of factors that increase a person's interest and make life interesting and challenging.

Structured data: Data that is collected in a uniform way.

Supportive relationship: An encounter between people that conveys warmth, understanding and sincerity.

U

Unstructured data: Data which is not tightly controlled by the interviewer, or by the questionnaire being completed. Such data is expressed in respondents' own words.

V

Vulnerability: Being at risk of some kind of harm – not being protected from risk and harm.

Index

A

abuse 15, 29, 47
access to services 37–9
accident and emergency
    departments 70–4
active lifestyle 107–8
adaptive/maladaptive
    behaviour 25–6
adult screening tests 125–8
    blood pressure for
        hypertension 125–6, 128
    eye tests 127–8
    mammography 128
    smear test for cervical
        cancer 126
    testicular cancer 128
adults 7, 107
advocacy 82, 85, 135
ageing population 34–5, 36
aggression, coping with 70–2
aggression prevention 70–1
alcohol and health 104, 106,
    109–10, 111, 113
alternative therapies 14
amniocentesis 121, 122, 128, 135
anaemia 122
anorexia nervosa 106, 109
antenatal screening 121–2
    amniocentesis 121, 122, 128,
        135
    blood tests 121, 122, 128
    CVS 121–2, 128
antibiotics 116
antibodies 114, 115, 135
antigens 114, 135
anti-discriminatory practices 2
anxiety 108
aphasia 56, 58
approval/praise 2, 4, 30
assertion 70–1, 72
atheroma 106
attention-seeking 20
attitudes and prejudices 18, 23,
    62
autism 68
autonomy 2, 3, 135

B

babies and infants 4–5, 9, 10,
    12, 32
    screening tests 122–5
balanced diet 104–6, 113
Bales's categories (1970) 63–4
barriers
    internal to carers 18–20, 21
    to service access 37–9
    see also service user barriers
behavioural difficulties and
    education 36
benefits of exercise 6
blood groupings 122
blood tests 121, 122–3, 128
blood-borne viruses 42–3, 135
body language/posture 23,
    52–5, 61, 74
Bordetella pertussis 116
Braille 57, 135
British Deaf Association 56
British Sign Language (BSL) 56,
    57, 69, 81, 85, 135
bulimia 106, 109
bullying 16, 17, 21

C

calm in face of aggression 73,
    75
calorie intake 104
cancer 109, 126, 128
    fear of 112
    protection through exercise
        108
carbohydrates 104, 105, 106
caring presence 77
caring skills and techniques
    23–30
cervical smear 126, 128
challenge/targets 30
children 5, 7, 12, 15, 107
    screening tests 122–5
choice 2, 3, 15, 135
cholera 119, 120
chorionic villus sampling (CVS)
    121–2, 128, 135

Christian Scientists 120
Clostridium tetani 117
Committee on Medical Aspects
    of Food Policy (COMA)
communication as barrier to
    services 38–9
communication barriers 58–62,
    135, 137
    in specific settings 66–80
communication difficulties 56–7
    overcoming 56–7
communication skills 20, 49–96,
    135
communication, types of 50–5
community nursing 32
community psychiatric nurses
    32
community services 31
compliance 27–8
concealment of real needs 20
confidence, lack of 62
confidentiality 2, 4, 26, 135
conflict avoidance 27–30
congenital hypothyroidism
    (CH) 122–3
consultation, communication
    during 77–8
Control of Substances
    Hazardous to Health
    (COSHH) 11
coronary heart disease 109
coronary thrombosis 125
Corynebacterium diptheriae 116
counselling 27
crèches 34
cultural beliefs/assumptions as
    barrier 60–2, 135
cultural differences 20, 23

D

day care 35
day centres, communication in
    67
day nurseries 33–4
day surgery 31–2
dental examination 123, 128

Department of Health
  standards 42
depression 108, 109
developmental dysplasia of the
  hip 125, 128
diabetes 106
  type 1 109
  type 2 109
diphtheria 114, 116, 120
disabled people 7, 8, 30, 70 102
disease 103, 135
  chronic 107
  immunisation 114–20
  inherited 104
disengagement 27, 29 135
disorder/malfunction 103, 135
distressed people, coping with
  70–4
diversity see equality
Down's syndrome 121, 122
DPT (diphtheria, pertussis,
  tetanus) vaccine 114, 116, 117
dyslexia 68
dysplasia 68

E
early years communication 66,
  67
early years provision 33–4, 36
eating sensibly 104–6, 108, 113
effective communication 2, 3,
  23, 24–5, 49–96, 136
emotional abuse 47
emotional support 74–7
empowerment 78, 136
equality and diversity 2, 15
equitable treatment 2, 3, 136
European guidelines 44
exaggeration 20
exercise and fitness 4–8, 107–8,
  111, 113
eye contact 23, 28–9, 53, 87, 89
eye tests 123–4, 127–8

F
face-to-face interaction 54–5
facial expression 28–9, 53
facilitators/facilitation 82, 136
fats 104, 105
  reduction 105–6, 107
feedback research 91–3
  audience response 93, 94
  qualitative data 93, 96, 136
  quantitative data 91, 92, 96,
    136

questionnaires 91, 92, 94, 96
  structured data 91–2, 137
  unstructured data 93, 137
  see also giving a talk
fibre/roughage 104, 105, 106
financial abuse/exploitation 47
fitness 104, 107–8
food labelling 105
formal care services 31–3
fruit and vegetables 105

G
General Medical Council 117
gestures 55
giving a talk 81–90
  audience management 87–8,
    94
  delivery 85–7
  information collection 82, 94
  planning 83–5, 95
  self-management 89–90, 94
  topic selection 81–22
glaucoma 127
GP consultation, diagnosis and
  treatment 31

H
hand washing 11–12
Health and Safety at Work Act
  1974 (HASAWA) 11, 44
Health and Safety First Aid
  Regulations (1981) 11
health care teams 7
health, concepts of 100–3
  factors affecting 104–13
health visitors 32
hearing impairment 69
hearing tests 124, 128
heart disease 106
hepatitis 43
  A 119, 120
high blood pressure 109
holistic concept of health 100–1,
  103, 136
home (domiciliary) care 35
hospital consultants 32
hospital infections 12, 44–5
hospital services 31–2
hospitals, communication in 67,
  74–7
hostile/obstructive behaviour 21
hostility 16, 17, 21, 62
housework 8
human immunodeficiency virus
  (HIV) 42–3, 118

hygiene 5, 11–12
hypertension 125–6, 136
hyperthyroidism 109

I
ignorance as barrier to services
  38, 39
ill health 103
illness 103, 136
immunisation 114–20
  programmes 116–20
  risks 117
immunity 114–20, 136
  active 114–15, 120, 135
  acquired 114–16, 135
  innate 114, 136
  passive 114, 115, 120, 136
inadequate resource/funding
  37, 39
individual rights 2
infant and child screening
  112–5, 128
  blood tests 112–3, 128
  dental 123, 128
  eye tests 123–4, 128
  hearing 124, 128
  hip dislocation 125, 128
informal care services 33–6
informal speech 58, 59
insecurity 15
Ishihara chart 124

J
Jehovah's Witnesses 120

L
life changes 4
life quality factors 2–14
  physical 4–14
  psychological 1–4
lifting injuries see manual
  handling
Lifting Operations and Lifting
  Equipment Regulations (1998)
  44
linguistic barriers 58–9
listening 14, 24, 74, 75, 76,
  78–80, 135
lymphocytes 114, 115, 136

M
Makaton 56–7, 136
malaria 119–20
mammography 128

Management of Health and Safety at Work Regulations (1992) 11, 44
manual handling 11, 44–5
Manual Handling Regulations (1992) 11, 44
measles 114, 116-17, 118, 120
medical advice 104, 112–13
medication for pain relief 14
methicillin-resistant *Staphylococcus aureus (MRSA)* 12, 43–4, 136
minerals 104, 105
miscarriage 122
MMR (triple) vaccine 117–18
mobility 8, 70
    problems and weight 106, 109
modelling 29, 136
monitoring for health 104, 108–9, 113
    see also screening
motivation, lack of 19
mumps 113, 120
muscle tension 55

N
National Advisory Committee for Nutrition Education (NACNE) 105
National Health Service (NHS) 7, 117
needs assessment 35
negative concept of health 100, 101, 103
negative feelings and behaviour 27–30
neglect 15–16, 17, 21, 47, 136
NHS Direct 32–3
    Wales 32
The NHS Plan 40–1
NHS services 31, 36
NHS24 (Scotland) 33
non-verbal communication 51–5, 75
    body language 52–5
    para language 51–2
nursery schools 34
nursing homes 34–5
    communication in 67
nutrients 104
nutrition 5, 8–10

O
obesity 105, 109
observation 24
occupation 2–3, 136
older people 3, 8, 10, 11, 15, 17, 34–5, 109
    cognitive function 108
    communicating with 78–80
    exercise 106
oral communication *see* verbal
osteo-arthritis 109
overweight people and problems 106, 109

P
pain, freedom from 5, 14
perception 23
Person Centred Planning 82, 89, 136
personal beliefs and identity 2
phagocytes 114
phenylketonuria (PKU) 122–3, 128
physical abuse 15, 47
physical comfort 5, 12–13
physical contact 27, 29
physical difficulties as barrier to services 38, 39
physical inactivity 107, 108
physical life quality factors 4–14
physical safety 5, 10–11
Plasmodium 119
playgroups 34
positive concept of health 100, 101, 103
post-natal depression 16
poverty and health 104
prejudices *see* attitudes
premature death 108, 109
pre-occupation with own needs 19
primary services 31
pro-active 24
professional referral 37
proof of identity 11
proteins 104, 105, 106
proximity and personal space 53–4
psychological abuse 47
psychological life quality factors 2–4
psychological security 2, 4, 136
punishment 16, 17, 21

R
rabies 119, 120
RCN guidelines 44
recall service 37
referral 31, 39
reflective caring 23, 24, 27, 137
rejection 16, 17, 21
relationship problems 16
Reporting of Injuries, Diseases and Dangerous Occurrences Regulations (1985) (RIDDOR) 11
residential homes 34–5
respect and value 73–4
respiratory difficulties 106
responsibilities *see* rights
rights and responsibilities 2
risks and safe working 42–7
Royal Association for Deaf People 56
rubella/German measles 118, 120

S
safety procedures *see* Health and Safety
salt in food 105, 106
screening for disease 120–8
    adults 125–8
    antenatal 121–2
    infant and child 122–5
secondary services 31
self-advocacy 82, 137
self-directed support 82, 88, 137
self-esteem 4, 15, 75, 137
self-referral 31, 37
sensory impairment 69
service user barriers 18, 20–1, 23
services available 31–6
    formal 31–3
    informal 33–6
sexual abuse 47
Sheridan-Gardner test 123, 124
sincerity/genuineness 75, 76–7
skill evaluation *see* feedback research
skill, lack of 20
sleep disorders 108
Snellen chart 124, 127
social contact 2, 3, 137
social perception 23, 137
social services 35

social support 2, 3, 137
special educational settings, communication in 67
special needs provision 35–6
specific learning difficulties 68–9
speech disability 69
spina bifida 122
sports 7
status/power, lack of 20
stereotyping 18–19, 137
stimulation 2, 3, 137
stress 108
strokes 106, 109, 125
sugar in food 105, 106
support within mainstream schools 36
supporting service users 23–5, 137
syndrome 118

T

team norms 65
teamwork and communication 63–5
tertiary services 31
tetanus/lockjaw 114, 117, 120
thalassaemia 122, 123, 128
therapy services 31
third-party referral 37
tobacco 104, 106, 110–12, 113
toxins 114, 116, 117, 136
training 20
translation/interpretation 59
travellers and vaccination 118–20
treating people well/badly 15–21
treatment and well-being 104, 112–13
triggers of aggression 72–3
trust 15, 26, 74, 75
tuberculosis 109
Tuckman's theory of group development (1965) 64–5
typhoid fever 119, 120

U

ulcer pain 109
understanding/empathy 75, 76
unfair discrimination 3, 17, 19, 21

V

vaccination *see* immunisation
verbal/oral communication 50
violence 11, 17, 21, 45–6
visual impairment 69
vitamins 104, 105
voice tone/pitch/clarity 51–2

W

warmth/acceptance 75–6
water and health 104, 105
weight and health 104, 106, 108–9
weight loss 109
well-being 101, 103
    factors affecting 104–13
whooping cough/pertussis 114, 120
winning and losing the argument 71, 72
workplace norms 19
World Health Organisation 100, 101, 117
written communication 51